JOHN WHITE

MAGNIFICENT OBSESSION

THE
JOY
OF
CHRISTIAN
COMMITMENT

*With Study Questions
for Individuals or Groups*

INTERVARSITY PRESS
DOWNERS GROVE, ILLINOIS 60515

InterVarsity Press is the book-publishing division of InterVarsity Christian Fellowship, a student movement active on campus at hundreds of universities, colleges and schools of nursing. For information about local and regional activities, write Public Relations Dept., InterVarsity Christian Fellowship, 6400 Schroeder Rd., P.O. Box 7895, Madison, WI 53707-7895.

Distributed in Canada through InterVarsity Press, 860 Denison St., Unit 3, Markham, Ontario L3R 4H1, Canada.

All Scripture quotations, unless otherwise indicated, are from the Holy Bible, New International Version. Copyright © 1973, 1978, International Bible Society. Used by permission of Zondervan Bible Publishers.

Discussion questions by Cindy Bunch.

Cover photograph: Robert McKendrick

ISBN 0-8308-1274-1

Printed in the United States of America ∞

_____

Library of Congress Cataloging-in-Publication Data
White, John, 1924 Mar. 5-
    Magnificent obsession: the joy of Christian commitment/John
White.
      p.   cm.
    Rev. ed. of: The cost of commitment. c1976.
    Includes bibliographical references.
    ISBN 0-8308-1274-1
    1. Christian life—1960-   2. Suffering—Religious aspects—
Christianity.   3. White, John, 1924 Mar. 5-   I. White, John, 1924
Mar. 5- Cost of commitment.   II. Title.
BV4510.2.W47   1990
248.4—dc20   90-32687
                              CIP

_____

16	15	14	13	12	11	10	9	8	7	6	5	4	3	2	1
99	98	97	96	95	94	93	92	91	90						

To Lorrie

Preface

I believe it was Han Suyin, the famous Chinese novelist, who pointed to the fact that there are two kinds of writers—those who research facts and arrange them in an appealing and logical fashion, and those who write from their experience of the same facts. It is the latter who experience truth, and write out of the depth of their struggles with it.

I have always wanted to be the second kind of writer. To grapple with truth within one's own body and in the depths of one's own being can and should be a lifelong goal. What else is life about? But in the course of that lifelong struggle, the struggler's perspective slowly changes. Horizons widen, hidden subtleties emerge, new perils and new glories reveal themselves.

Often I am asked whether I still am satisfied with things I wrote years ago. The question is hard to answer, since I rarely read my own books. For one thing there are many better books I need to read, and for another, like agonized writers of Ph.D. theses, I am usually so relieved to get a book out of my hair that I am glad to see the last of it. I like to spend a week or two recovering and then get on with something new.

But from time to time major dissatisfactions sweep over me, and I find myself saying, "How I wish I knew that *then*! I really ought to change (this or that) book."

Of course new fashions become current, new errors are promulgated, and books become dated. The situation which a book once addressed might no longer exist. Many books go out of fashion simply because they flog dead horses. Since this book was written, the health and wealth gospel has made significant strides—as it was bound to do in a culture devoted to pain-free comfort, fulfillment and financial prosperity. But its teachings need to be faced in a book about Christian sacrifice.

My book on the topic was originally entitled *The Cost of Commitment*. I felt passionately about commitment to Christ when I wrote it, and my passion has grown with the years. Mine was not a temporary, youthful enthusiasm. I might never have realized this had not my editors suggested I take another look at the original book. But if my passion has grown, so has my understanding of both the joys and the perils of commitment. Its cost today seems greater than ever. All this is reflected in what I now write.

And the backdrop against which we are to play out our commitment has changed. The issues are more numerous. Our public image, for example, has been blotched by major scandals in the lives of TV evangelists and others. We sometimes say they have sullied the name of Christ, but that name cannot be sullied. Even the hostile public entertains respect for Christ himself. However, TV evangelists have made it a shade more embarrassing for the rest of us to confess his name, knowing the response might be, "Oh, you're one of *them*, are you?"

The political climate has changed. Evil is more widely accepted, and Christian liberty in the West more easily eroded.

And the Christian scene itself has changed. For two or three decades we have been into "Christ-as-comforter," "Christ-as-psychological-soother" and "Christ-as-purveyer-of-riches," all without a corresponding emphasis on the crucified Christ who calls us to follow him even to prison and execution. So I have added a chapter on how Christians should view government and whether or not we should be involved in civil disobedience.

A new first chapter brings you up to date on my own life of commitment since I first wrote this book. And chapter nine adds some thoughts on faith in the face of spiritual warfare. Other new material is added here and there to round out the discussion, and I have reorganized the whole to make it flow more smoothly.

So I have sounded some new notes in this little book, which hopefully still blend with the older notes. I think you will find more passion rather than less—for I feel more deeply. And the passion must be passion for Christ, passion that transcends—without compromising—national and denominational loyalties.

Finally, I wanted to change the title. The original book was less about the cost of commitment to Christ than about the glory of it, the wonder and exciting privilege of it. I thought of *Commitment* as a title, but was not satisfied. As I reflected on the pearl merchant and his insane desire to sacrifice everything he had to possess one great pearl, I used the phrase *magnificent obsession*.

The editors suggested it might work as a title. And it does. For that is what I want to say more than anything. Commitment to Christ is commitment to the pursuit of the ultimate treasure. To sell all of our miserable bits and pieces is no sacrifice at all when he himself has become the consuming passion of our lives.

1

Recommitment

I *t is a lovely May evening. Through my study window I have been* watching, as evening falls, the fractured snow-covered surfaces of the Cascade Mountains slowly turn from white through gold to pink and shades of blue-gray.

I am sixty-five. And I can hardly believe it.

Sometimes I feel it, but more often I don't. I have been reminded of my age, during the past five years, whenever a clerk has asked, "Are you a senior citizen, sir?" At once I am reduced to irrelevance and feebleness. Whoever would want to be a senior citizen? I may be sixty-five, but I don't enjoy being categorized. I'm *me.* Oh, I know. They have to ask, and they generally ask kindly. I should not react as I do. I still have lessons to learn.

But that is just my point. I'm still learning, learning new things— exciting things about life, about myself, about—well, everything. I'm still changing, still *becoming.* I am an old dog learning new tricks.

It can be dismaying and disappointing, of course. At times I find myself filled with regret and a sense of loss. I keep saying, "Oh, if only I had known (this or that) forty years ago! How different life might have been!" But I can't ever let the dismay overwhelm me. For one thing, I see the frightening spectacle of many of my peers who for years have stagnated in routines and have stopped growing. In some sense they even seem to have stopped living. They react like aging editions of what they were as youths, not more mature so much as more dull, youths with no fire left, more cautious, more rigid. I'm less in touch with them than I used to be. But on the other hand I find new friends among people less than half my age who happen to be learning some of the same things I myself am learning. Perhaps this more than anything preserves a youthful disposition in me.

My body is aging. I creak here and there, I tire more easily, I sometimes sleep poorly, and I eat less. When I get out of the shower and see my reflection in the mirror, I realize I'm not Michelangelo's *David*—indeed, I never was. I'm almost bald and I'm the wrong shape. But despite the reminders of the approaching grave, I am being renewed inside constantly.

I'm motivated—most of the time. It may be harder to learn new things. Occasionally I even rebel. But on the whole I have greater desires to learn—more hope, more push than when I was younger.

And I think I know why. It has to do with *commitment.* For commitment, real commitment, can carry you beyond the aging process in spite of degenerative changes. Age need not always be a dull descent into apathy and decrepitude. Something is happening inside me that refuses to let me lie down and vegetate.

I experience more than I used to—stronger emotional pain and greater joy. I'm more intensely alive, more in love with my wife, more awed by creation and more spellbound before any newborn child. And it goes back to something that happened when I took an early retirement over six years ago from both psychiatric practice and academic life. (Although, the process has really been going on since I was sixteen.) Let me say again that I still feel my age, but the life inside me refuses to be suppressed by my aging body.

Paradise Tarnished

I retired because the demands of writing books began to compete with the psychiatric and academic sides of my life, and I had to choose one or the other. After praying about the matter for a year or two, my wife, Lorrie, and I decided I should opt for writing. So we bought a fairly isolated condominium on the shore of a large lake that had several thousand islands. There I could write in solitude.

It was gorgeous. There was the matter of four months of snow, of course, winter blizzards and subzero temperatures. But winter in the country is spectacular, and all necessary snow-clearing was done for us. The snow itself always remained clean and white. We had central heating for warmth and even a plentiful supply of firewood which was cut and stacked for us.

As for the other seasons, each had its special joy. For me the year or so we spent by the lake was a time of healing. The rush of the city, the grueling pace of practice, and the pettiness of academic life were all replaced by the call of loons, the chatter of squirrels and the sight of pinewoods and islands on a lake. I would walk through the woods and let their peace soak into me. In the winter I would trudge for miles across the hard frozen lake. And in the summer I would swim, sometimes again for miles, in the thirty-inch sun-warmed layer of water that rested above the wintry cold of the deeper waters of the lake.

And, of course, I would write and study and pray.

But gradually my paradise began to seem less attractive. Something was missing. For instance, I noticed that the woods were not perfect. It was partly because Lorrie was not able to walk very far and could not accompany me very often, but at a deeper level I was bothered by the decay and death mixed with the beauty, spoiling it to some degree by reminding me that I was surrounded by an earth that had been cursed.

There was also a growing feeling of a deeper struggle in life than that which I was experiencing. We were active in Christian work; my writing seemed to be owned by God. Yet I could not shake the feeling that we were in a sort of back water. Later I remembered Shakespeare's *Henry VIII:*

There is a tide in the affairs of men, Which taken at the flood leads on to fortune; Omitted, all the voyage of their life Is bound in shallows and in miseries.[1]

In escaping from the rat race, had we somehow drifted into "shallows and miseries"? I wanted to be part of a battle.

I began to ask God to take me right to the battlefront. I wasn't asking for glory or for the spotlight, only for a life that would matter, right to its end. I was hungry for something. Yet, though the battle was part of it, indeed a big part, it went even deeper. I wanted to be where the Lord himself was most in evidence.

One day Lorrie said to me, "You know, I've been praying for some time about something."

"You have? What have you been praying about?"

"I'm not happy here, John."

"I know. It's rough on you. You're a people person and

we're a bit cut off here. You don't even see much of me. I'm sorry, honey, it's not much fun for you. When I'm not typing, I'm out walking alone."

"But it's more than that. I feel so useless. *I want to be where the battle is.*"

My remorse suddenly turned to joy. "You too? I've been praying that for months. I want to die with my boots on."

So we began to pray together for an assignment at the front line of the battle—wherever that might prove to be for us. We did not fully realize it, but we were recommitting ourselves to God. For commitment is never a static thing. It tends to wane. From time to time we need a new vision and a renewal of our vows, a new decision to follow fully, to the death if need be.

At first nothing changed, but we went on praying for we knew what we wanted. Then a few weeks later a telephone call from a friend opened a door that led to our exploring new avenues. Gradually, as our commitment was implemented in day-to-day obedience, the sense of new life which we recognized from previous times of refreshing began to quicken our spirits again. Later still, we sold the condominium and for three years lived out of suitcases. But that is another story.

Sorrow and Joy

Our renewed commitment has brought pain and sorrow as well as joy. It has even pulled out of the woodwork sins and weaknesses we were unaware of, as well as others we had never dealt with properly. Among the pains and sorrows have been some we recognize from our past Christian experience (loss of friends, criticism) and at least one new kind of distress.

A year or so ago in another country, I found myself praying for a dear friend, a citizen of that country. As I prayed, the

Lord seemed to be speaking to me. "This man will be put to death for me not too long in the future." I tried to suppress the voice. I was disturbed and stumbled in my praying. My prayer seemed unreal.

Two days later I watched one of the team members who accompanied me as he prayed for the same man. Suddenly, he burst into tears, weeping pitifully as he struggled to pray on. "Why did you weep?" I asked him later.

"While I was praying, the Lord told me that our friend is going to be a martyr," he said.

Perhaps it shouldn't cause us sorrow. Instead, we should be awed and full of rejoicing for the glory of it. After all, there are casualties in real battles, and martyrs get special crowns. Why does God trust us with such knowledge? Our thoughts are not yet God's thoughts, and we cling to those whom we love. Every time I look at my friend I weep a little inside. I lack the courage to tell him. But perhaps I will someday soon. Just now I can't face it.

Suffering and sorrow. What role do they play in a life of commitment? Why should they be a part of following Christ? Both are part of commitment and in chapters five, six and seven I'll talk more about this, and about how to distinguish suffering for Jesus from suffering because of our sin, our stupidity and our folly.

I also weep tears which have nothing to do with pain. Some months ago, after ministering with a team in Hong Kong, Philemon Choi and his wife took us on a trip to Macau, the Portuguese colony on the Chinese coast. We had set out early so that it was still morning when Pastor Lam, a former Hong Kong football star and a power for the gospel in Macau, took us to the church James Morrison built years ago. We visited his grave and saw the graves of his wife and of his children, many of whom died very young.

I stood silently at the foot of Morrison's grave and began to sob. I did not understand why I was sobbing. I had never met Morrison; indeed, he died long before I was born. I had not even thought about him for years. I wept episodically all that day. I had only to think about Morrison's grave and I would start to cry again. I tried to talk about it once or twice, but I had to give up because I would wind up weeping. What was happening to me?

It was only later that I understood. I had read about James Morrison many years before, moved by the role he had played in the evangelization of China, by his translations and by the Chinese dictionary he produced. His role had been highly significant in the earliest days of Protestantism in China. But what was it that so moved me?

The Portuguese have a word for it—*saudade*. It has to do with the deepest longings of your heart. And my longing was to be where the battle was, where Jesus was, and to experience the reality of God himself. In some mysterious fashion the solidness and reality of Morrison's grave had brought me into contact with the greater reality I longed for. As I touched the gravestone and read its inscription, God reached through and released intense longings so deep within me that I had not realized they were even there.

I have news for you. You have those same longings. Buried, perhaps, and hidden from your consciousness, but waiting to be awakened. It's Augustine all over again. There is a tug and a hunger buried in our hearts, an unease that will never be satisfied until God's purposes for us are fulfilled. It will stay there until our hearts find rest in the God who placed it there. The finding may be sudden or gradual, perhaps more likely in a series of clamberings and crises, until we are altogether committed to him.

C. S. Lewis writes about this in his book *The Pilgrim's Regress*.

In chapter two he describes John's experience when he catches a glimpse of incomparable loveliness through a window with no bars. "There came to him from beyond the wood a sweetness and a pang so piercing that instantly he forgot his father's house, and his mother, and the fear of the Landlord, and the burden of the rules. All the furniture of his mind was taken away. A moment later he found that he was sobbing. . . . It seemed to him that a mist which hung at the far end of the wood had parted for a moment, and through the rift he had seen a calm sea, and in the sea an island."[2]

From that point John's life becomes a pursuit of the island he saw in the vision. We think of total commitment to God as austere, sacrificial and joyless. But in Lewis's story of John's quest, the contrast lies between the vision of beauty for which he hungered and two other things—the confusing rules of the mysterious and demanding Landlord, and the spurious pleasures John was offered on his journey. Both were false substitutes for the island. Commitment has nothing to do with the bondage of religious "oughts." Nor can its joys be compared with the satisfactions we pursue so ardently. Commitment has to do with the pursuit of God himself. It is a being drawn and pulled. It is becoming what we were designed to be, what we truly are, and doing what we were designed and meant to do. I discuss this a little in chapter nine.

Sorrow and pain there may be, even humiliation, but the joys are incomparable. A couple of weeks after the incident at James Morrison's grave, Ellen, Philemon Choi's wife, accompanied a few of us to Guangzhou (formerly Canton), the capital of Guangdong Province in mainland China. There we met another Pastor Lam, a sixty-year-old man who cares for a house church of eight hundred members. His house was on a narrow street that admitted only pedestrians and bicycles.

Even though the church was not government approved and not supposed to exist, people in the street, seeing we were foreigners, asked us whether we were looking for Lam's house and volunteered to show us where it was. Inside that shell of a house, smiling young people hurried to bring us tea.

Lam had been imprisoned twice for his faith. His second imprisonment had lasted twenty-five years, doing hard labor in the mines. I asked him how he felt about it, and joy poured out of him. "It was wonderful!" he cried. "I could have been killed many times, but God preserved my life. And I wasn't injured in the mine, even though men around me were maimed and killed. I even preached there!"

He spoke fairly good English and described something of his life to us. But the story, fascinating as it was, was hard to concentrate on, so amazed were we by the extraordinary joy that filled and overflowed from him. Three times the police had been to interrogate him during the previous two weeks, but he had laughed with genuine merriment. "I will preach!" he cried. "They can only take me if the Lord lets them. And I will go on preaching about Jesus wherever I am!" It was not bravado. It was a quality of joy we had never encountered before.

As we thought about the threats to his safety and his astounding courage, we were humbled and amazed. He had found the treasure that surpasses all else in his commitment to Jesus. Christ is that treasure. In the next chapter I will explore how commitment to Christ leads to pain and sorrow, but also to joy unspeakable and full of glory.

As for me, I'm hooked. I'm committed now, not because I'm a superior Christian, but because I've become an addict. I know what I want, and I want what I want. His hook is in my jaw, and it's painful but it's also ecstasy to be pulled.

Questions for Individuals or Groups

1. To what does the author attribute his ability to grow and change even as he ages (p. 14)?

2. How does commitment make you more open to learning what God has for you? When has a lack of commitment caused you to miss an opportunity from God?

3. What was it that the author missed when he moved to an isolated area to write (pp. 16-17)? Describe what he means by this term.

4. Have you ever been at a point when your commitment to the Christian life was standing still? What did you do to move forward again?

5. How is it that the commitment which the author says brings him such joy also brings him sorrow? Have you ever felt that pain mixed with joy because of your commitment to Christ? Explain.

6. On pages 18-19 the author says that his longing to live a life in the battlefield, as James Morrison did, moved him to tears when he saw Morrison's grave. What are the deep longings of your heart? (If you are unsure, how could you identify those feelings?)

7. Describe the false substitutes for commitment which are found in the excerpt from *The Pilgrim's Regress* (p. 20). What are some other possible substitutes? How have you seen them affecting your spiritual life?

8. Summarize commitment according to the author's description of it in this chapter. What does commitment mean to you personally?

2

The Way
of the
Cross

I f we want to be committed to Jesus, devoting our lives to following him, we must radically change the way we view our lives. We must look both at our own lives and at the world through the eyes of Christ. Things which once mattered greatly will cease to matter. Other things once thought of as having no consequence will seem paramount.

But how do we look through the eyes of Christ? How did Christ himself see the world? How did he view his own life? What were his values? What was his goal in life? What did he see as his own future?

His goal was to know the will of the Father and to do it. It was his aim both because he loved the Father and because he loved us. In consequence, Christ lived a life shadowed by the awareness that an early death awaited him. In doing the Father's will, he would be cut down as a man in his prime. To redeem the world he loved, he knew he faced a criminal's death, a violent and shameful death. Late in his public ministry, he even knew precisely when this would take place.

Yet, paradoxically, his outlook on life was positive and joyous, not in spite of the awful shadow so much as *because* of it. The shame of the cross was something he despised, knowing that it was not only to prove a supreme triumph but that it would win him the object of his love. The writer to the Hebrews makes this clear when he writes about a "Jesus . . . who for the joy set before him endured the cross, scorning its shame . . ."

I do not mean that he experienced neither horror nor agony. He experienced both. But he chose the cross because it was the price he had to pay for something that was supremely important to him. The price might be incredibly high, higher than for anything else ever bought, yet Christ determined to get what he wanted.

What was it he wanted? He wanted to please the Father and he wanted us. Think of it. Father, Son and Holy Spirit want fellowship with us. For Christ the cost was worth the bargain. You may not feel that fellowship with you is worth much, but Christ values your fellowship very highly indeed.

We make a great mistake then when we pity Christ on the cross. Astonishment—Yes! Wonder and amazement—Yes! Adoration and awe—Yes! Even tears. But pity—Never!

I am not suggesting that we take Christ's death lightly. If for no other reason than the unparalleled love for us his death represents, we can only regard it with the utmost wonder and solemnity. That came home to me on a plane ride to Virginia Beach.

The seat next to me was empty, but there was a man in the aisle seat, and people on the seats immediately behind and in front of me. I was praying silently so that my neighbors would not realize I was praying, and as I did so I sensed the Holy Spirit prompting me to meditate on the death of Christ. Immediately, I could see with my mind's eye a picture of the naked Christ hanging in pain. Then the strange thing occurred. The Spirit said, "Look into his eyes!"

In my mind I said, "How do I know I'll not just be playing a psychological game with myself?"

For a moment there was no answer, and then came the repeated command, "Look into his eyes."

I did so—and his eyes burned tender love into mine, looking down at me from across the seatbacks ahead of me. It was totally unexpected. I have never encountered so powerful a love. It shocked me. And then the eyes spoke—I cannot explain what I mean by that; it just was so. Silently, but with precision and clarity they said, "I'm so glad to be doing this for you!"

I dropped my head, unable to face those eyes or the power of that kind of love a moment longer. Forgetting my neighbors, I cried out loud, "I can't stand it! Jesus! Jesus!" The force of what was communicated was too much to bear. I knew I should have gone on looking, but I could not face love of that intensity and quality. I was ashamed and humbled, yet filled with the longing that I might go back there someday to finish what was interrupted. Later, I glanced surreptitiously at the man in the aisle seat, but he seemed too absorbed by his book to have been bothered by my cry which the noise of the engines may have absorbed.

The more I meditate on the death of Christ, the more awesome it seems. But if I am sure of one thing, it is that it does not call for pity so much as for wonder and amazement at the greatest achievement in human history by the strongest and holiest man in history, the God-man. It was the supreme achievement of love, carried out for a joy that lay ahead. And we are called to commitment, to follow him along the way of the cross, to "fix our eyes on Jesus."

Wrong Views about the Way of the Cross

Obviously, we are not all going to die a violent and shameful death at the age of thirty-three. What we will do, if we view life as Christ did, is to regard everything else in life, even life itself, as secondary to serving the Father. But in attempting to come to grips with commitment, Christians have made serious mistakes by failing to grasp the positive emphasis of commitment. Terms such as "sacrificial living" and "the way of the cross" conjure visions of hollow-cheeked earnestness. Their emphasis lies on doing without. It is as though the more you do without, and the more you suffer, the more spiritual your brand of Christianity is.

This "negative" view represents part of the truth. What we are going to talk about will indeed involve going without. But as we shall see, self-denial and pain are less than half the story. Indeed, to stress the negative at the expense of the positive—the losses rather than the gains—represents a serious distortion of the truth.

It does more than distort truth. It presents formidable spiritual hurdles for the person who seeks to put it into practice. If we consciously deny ourselves something we like, we find ourselves battling an exalted view of our own spirituality. Our struggle is complicated by the fact that we have indeed done (as we see it) something virtuous. Something within us demands recognition.

We can tell ourselves as many times as we like that we "only did it by God's grace" or that it was "God's work within" us and not our own work at all. The fact of the matter is that it is our work. Though we were sincere in our sacrifice, it may well have represented self-effort, self-effort we try to palm off on the Holy Spirit in a futile struggle to stay humble.

It is also hard not to feel critical of people who seem less dedicated. Naturally, we don't want to be Pharisees, so we will do our best to suppress critical feelings. But we won't be able to help them. They arise from a mistaken notion of what it is to follow Christ closely. Christians place so much emphasis on what committed Christians must avoid that it's important to tackle some of these common errors.

The way of the cross is not a denial of the value of intellectual activity. Some Christians say to me, "We don't believe in higher education. It is worldly." But it is not higher education that is worldly, only ambitions of better jobs and prestige or intellectual and academic snobbery. It is true that knowledge puffs up, and it is true that many Christians lose out because of their academic ambitions, but these dangers arise not when we pursue, but when we prostitute, learning. Nothing in Scripture cancels the advice for us to "get knowledge, get understanding." In Christ's army, scholars and carpenters march shoulder to shoulder. No calling gets a higher rating than any other. It is our motive in pursuing the calling, whether academic or manual, that matters.

The way of the cross is not a denial of the value of artistic expression. Insofar as human nature is corrupt, creativity can be put to corrupt uses. Had you been a Hebrew in Joshua's day, you would have had to destroy pictures and statues captured in battle. You would have destroyed them because you were vulnerable to raw idolatry and demonism, living in an age in which the belief in evil deities and in their dwelling in images was strong. Modern archaeologists and art historians might weep over the "priceless" treasures lost to posterity, but your responsibility at that point in history was to preserve something of greater value for posterity—the knowledge of the one true God, who did not dwell in images made by humans. The loss of archaeological artifacts was a small price to pay to keep that of far greater worth.

Whether every puritanical assault upon the visual arts was justified, I cannot say. I raise the point because many devoted Christians for one reason or another have regarded all artistic expression as suspect except the composition of "Christian" music, hymnwriting and the writing of Christian novels and such. Without realizing it, many Christians measure spirituality in terms of cultural and artistic impoverishment, which is hardly what God intended.

The One whose creative genius gave us the awesome spectacle of stellar galaxies and the fragile beauty of snow crystals and orchids made us to be, like him, creators too. The danger of art is that we begin to worship artistic expression itself, instead of receiving it thankfully from his hands or giving it to him in worship. And for that danger we must always watch.

Therefore, you will not be sharing Christ's sufferings by putting your Beethoven records away forever, if Beethoven is what you like, unless there is a good reason to do so.

The way of the cross is not a denial of the rightness of pleasure. God invented pleasure. God gave it to the human race. The devil only taught us how to misuse it; he adulterated pleasure with evil, making it sinful pleasure. But the fact that some abuse pleasure is no reason for the people of God to abandon it—leaving the impression that pleasure is the devil's concession.

However, pleasure must never become lust. Lust is born when pleasure becomes an end in itself, or when pursuing pleasure becomes more important to you than obeying God.

Christians find it hard to hold this truth in balance. It is so much easier to label certain pleasures evil—to say, for example, that sex apart from intended procreation is evil; that movies, novels, dancing, alcohol, tobacco, secular music are taboo; but that playing orchestral arrangements of pretty hymn tunes is virtuous and spiritual. It simplifies the whole question. And on the face of it the approach seems sound. For instance, so much in the movies and on TV is not only garbage but is diabolical garbage.

But we pay a price for such simplistic thinking. If all we were to sacrifice was the enjoyment of God-given delights, the price would be small. However to the degree that we see our faith in negative terms we will, wittingly or unwittingly, so present it. Worse still, whatever we preach to the contrary, we will feel deep down inside us that if we observe the cardinal no-no's of evangelicalism, we are being faithful followers of Christ. In fact, our lives may be empty not only of pleasure but also of godliness. Satan will then have gained a major victory in us.

Soldiers in wartime must forego pleasure, not because pleasure is evil (though some pleasures are), but because more pressing claims demand their attention. They may spend bitter months hungry and thirsty, dressed in foul-smelling clothes, with eyes sore with wakefulness, feet blistered and limbs craving rest.

Yet their leaders know the value not only of food and rest but of recreation. They see to it that furloughs are given with an opportunity for the pleasures they have been denied.

Christians are called to warfare. The times we live in will not be normal until Christ returns to reign. Pressing duties demand that we endure hardships and forego pleasure.

Yet at times our heavenly captain will heap upon us not only spiritual delights but, because we have physical bodies, physical delights as well. As followers of Christ, we are not called to pursue pleasure but to follow our leader. Yet we need not be discomfited by the showers of delight he occasionally surprises us with, even in times of war.

So far I have been explaining what the way of the cross is not. Since I have pleaded with you to see it in positive not in negative terms, it is time I did so myself. In positive terms the way of the cross is: first, the discovery of incomparable treasure at the cost of everything else in life and, second, the discovery of freedom at the price of selling myself into slavery.

The Incomparable Treasure

"The kingdom of heaven is like a treasure hidden in a field. When a man found it, he hid it again, and then in his joy he went and sold all he had and bought that field" (Mt 13:44).

No details are given in this story except for the man's emotional state. He has discovered treasure buried in a field. How did he find it? Was he employed by the owner of the field? We do not know.

We know only three things. He covered the treasure up; he was delirious with joy; he was so excited that he sold everything he possessed in order to buy the field.

Here is a picture of reckless sacrificing of all a man possesses. Yet it is clearly not so much a picture of renunciation as it is of re-evaluation.

Up to this point in his life the man has doubtlessly valued his possessions highly. Like all of us, he would have clung to them and only parted with them under exceptional circumstances. He might have lent to a neighbor in distress or sold something to help a close friend or relative. But by and large his life has consisted in the abundance of the things he possessed.

It is only when he discovers buried treasure that his perspective changes. Suddenly his possessions look cheap and paltry. A joy is rising in him and an excitement that makes him sweat and tremble. There may have been regret about a cherished piece of furniture or a family heirloom. But it is only momentary. The choice he faces lies between his worthless bits and pieces and the field with buried treasure. There is nothing noble about his sacrifice. There would, on the other hand, be something incredibly stupid about not making it. Anyone but a fool would do exactly as the man did. Everyone will envy him for his good fortune and commend him not on his spiritual character, but on his common sense.

What I have called "his miserable bits and pieces" are the things of this life to which we naturally cling—money, property, cars, prestige or a good job. Jesus is not telling us that we must sacrifice all our possessions to inherit heavenly treasure, only that if we were to grasp what glories he has for us we would realize how silly we are to cling to such rubbish.

But we must be honest with ourselves. How important to us are possessions and ambitions? How real are heavenly treasures? John Bunyan's *Pilgrim's Progress* has in it what for me is an unforgettable picture. In one chapter the hero, Christian, visits the house of the Interpreter. One of the pictures he sees there portrays a man with a muckrake, grovelling in filth in the hope of what pickings he may find there. Christ offers him a crown, but he is so absorbed in what he is doing that he fails to see the crown above his head. We are like that man—so absorbed with straws and rags that we fail to see the glorious crown extended to us.

There is a magnificent insanity about the parable in Matthew 13:45. It has to do with a pearl freak—a merchant whose hobby was pearls. Evidently, one day he came across a pearl to end all pearls. Imagine him with staring eyes, quickly taking in his breath, licking his dry lips, then anxiously inquiring about price, haggling and pondering the tremendous cost of the pearl. You can also imagine him returning home and looking over the rest of his pearl collection. With shaking hands he would pick them up one by one and drop them into a soft leather pouch. Not only pearls, but house, slaves and everything would go so that the one pearl might become his.

And then, bereft of everything but a big pearl, what would the fool do? You can't eat pearls. In my mind is a picture of the crazy guy sitting in a miserable hovel—his glowing eyes feasting on his pearl and his fingers gently caressing it. Crazy? Perhaps he is the one sane person among us.

It all depends on whether the pearl was worth it. We see at once that treasure in heaven would be worth it. Why then are we so quick to opt for earthly treasure and so slow to be interested in the heavenly? Perhaps it is because we do not believe in heavenly realities. They represent a celestial cliché in our minds, but no more.

Only true faith will make us step along the way of the cross. And if we are to step lightheartedly, there will have to be the kind of faith which has become profound conviction that the joys are real and tangible, the next life is very important, and Jesus really is preparing a place on high.

The way of the cross is a magnificent obsession with a heavenly pearl, beside which everything else in life has no value. If it were a case of buying it, we would gladly sell all we had to do so.

But we cannot buy heavenly treasure. It is not for sale. The point of the parable is that having caught a glimpse of the pearl, we count all else of no value and pursue the treasure.

Again and again in my life I have had to face choices. At one stage in my life it was English literature or Jesus. Though I was a medical student, I had a passion for literature. I even tried to collect first editions of Victorian novelists. I read late into the night, so late that I would be no use the next day.

Good literature was an escape for me. I was not reading it as it should be read but drugging my mind in soporific clouds of words.

But God had shown me something of his own treasures, and my heart craved them. In some dim way I perceived that my weakness for fiction interfered with my capacity to experience the joys of Christ. So I packed all the works of eighteenth- and nineteenth-century novelists and poets into a great crate and gave them to a friend who was majoring in English.

I was left with a sense of relief and gratitude. I have never questioned the sanity of that decision. Today, books are crammed untidily on all my bookshelves and litter every room in my house. They no longer hinder me as they once did.

I suppose the choice I made was a sacrifice. Yet I saw it more in terms of what I longed for more—my pearl.

The choices facing us may be comparatively trivial or great. The same principle holds. Once when I was on a well-earned winter holiday, an idea gripped me as I lay sunning on the beach. I had paper and pen with me, so I rolled over and began to write. A breeze was fluttering and tearing the loose pages I held down on the sand. The sun's caressing warmth turned into a headaching glare. My position was uncomfortable. It would be much more sensible to go to my hotel room if I wanted to write. But I wanted a suntan to prove I had been on a winter holiday. I could not have it both ways. It was writing or tan. I chose writing.

My choice was not virtuous. It was simply a matter of what I wanted more. There were no "oughts" about it, though my choice may say something about my values.

Freedom through Slavery

That choice and similar choices have left me thankful because they have begun to set me free. For to be free means to be released from being torn in two directions at once. It means to have one passion only—one pearl of great price—rather than half a dozen conflicting passions. Let me quote to you a letter written by an American Communist in Mexico City, a letter breaking his engagement with his fiancée.

We communists suffer many casualties. We are those whom they shoot, hang, lynch, tar and feather, imprison, slander, fire from our jobs and whose lives people make miserable in every way possible. Some of us are killed and imprisoned. We live in poverty. From what we earn we turn over to the Party every cent which we do not absolutely need to live.

We communists have neither time nor money to go to movies very often, nor for concerts nor for beautiful homes and new cars. They call us fanatics. We are fanatics. Our lives are dominated by one supreme factor—the struggle for world communism. We communists have a philosophy of life that money could not buy.

We have a cause to fight for, a specific goal in life. We lose our insignificant identities in the great river of humanity; and if our personal lives seem hard or if our egos seem bruised through subordination to the Party, we are amply rewarded—in the thought that all of us, even though it be in a very small way, are contributing something new and better for humanity.

There is one thing about which I am completely in earnest—the communist cause. It is my life, my business, my religion, my hobby, my sweetheart, my wife, my mistress, my meat and drink. I work at it by day and dream of it by night. Its control over me grows greater with the passage of time. Therefore I cannot have a friend, a lover or even a conversation without relating them to this power that animates and controls my life. I measure people, books,

ideas and deeds according to the way they affect the communist cause and by their attitude to it. I have already been
in jail for my ideas, and if need be I am ready to face death.
If the letter fails to stir you, you may already have begun to
die. Like a traveler lost in a blizzard, unaware your body
freezes in a snowbank, you are drifting to sleep.

But if your heart beats more quickly—be glad. You have
hope of a more bracing life than the one most of us live. For
Christ did not call you to suburbia and a mortgage but to a
gallows and a crown of glory.

The unknown Communist in Mexico City startles us into
seeing how trivial our lives are. We may not share his opin-
ions. We may even be appalled at the abandon with which he
hurls all that is dear to him into the crushing presses of a
political machine. Yet we are glad to see a man who is willing
to commit his all and even to die for what he believes in—
however wrong he may be.

In reading the letter, you may also feel that he has been set
free. Having broken from the possessions that clutter our
own lives, he is consumed by a passion that despises both
prudence and pleasure. For the time, at least, lusts that plague
the rest of us seem to hold no attraction for him. Yet it is not
the sternness of his renunciation that comes through, so
much as an exhilarating sense of freedom.

His freedom has nothing to do with his political ideology.
It has to do with his being human, though fallen, released
from lesser passions by pursuit of greater ones. It is a freedom that may have awakened an echo in your own heart as
you read his letter. For you were not created, much less redeemed, to sell your birthright as Issac did for a mess of
pottage. You have been called to a still more radical commitment than his and to gamble your life on higher stakes.

"If anyone would come after me," Jesus again tells us, "he

must deny himself and take up his cross daily and follow me" (Lk 9:23).

The cross symbolizes our willingness to give up all else for the surpassing glory of following it, or to die if need be. Jesus calls us to pick it up and heave it over our backs—not to wear it in our lapels or round our necks, but to carry it over our shoulders—in the same way he carried his own cross. It may look rough and heavy as you stare at it on the ground, but you will be surprised to find how light it feels as you bear it. And it will mark you in the eyes of demons, men and angels as one who despises humiliation and who deliberately chooses the company of the One from whom the world hides its face.

For the popular Christ and the true Christ are two different Christs. The first is the watered-down Christ, remolded to please the masses. You may stand with that Christ and please as many people as he does. But the real Christ does not aim to please people so much as to love them and to glorify the Father. Jesus' truth pierced human consciences; his love frightened and alienated them, while his relentless pursuit of the Father's glory threatened the institutions they upheld. They could not tolerate his continued existence, and so they murdered him.

"Whoever serves me," Jesus once said, "must follow me; and where I am, my servant also will be" (Jn 12:26).

To stand where he stands, to walk in his steps means necessarily running the gauntlet of the attitudes that still slumber in human hearts, attitudes which will awaken the moment we step after him. He wants us to understand this clearly before we choose. For to choose to follow him will mean saying, as Paul said, "I consider my life worth nothing to me" (Acts 20:24). We will have to place on the table career, money, affections, ambitions, plans, hobbies and our very lives, and say: "It hurts me to place these here, but I know you can replace them a hundredfold. Let them be disposed of as they may—returned to me or lost forever. Their fate will not influence my choice. I want to follow you wholly." To do this is to be released from the chains that enslave people everywhere. It is also to take up our crosses and to replace a heavy burden with a light one. It is to be set free.

One night when I was sixteen, I was too excited to sleep. For the first time I saw the years of my life as a lump sum. Whereas many people spend their lives a few weeks at a time, squandering life aimlessly on whatever would catch their attention, I wanted to use the total sum of my years to purchase something big. Exciting fantasies swept over the screen of my imagination. Then, in a moment of wonder and gratitude, it occurred to me that I could hand my years in their entirety to Christ to be disposed of in whatever way he chose. I knelt by my bed and did so.

My decision was not a noble one. In part at least it was based on self-interest. Yet he mercifully took me at my word and brought me back to that same decision repeatedly. I did not realize at the time that there was nothing mechanical about the contract between us. I supposed that having handed my years to him I would have no further say in the matter, and that automatically he would take the years from me, since they were his.

And so they were. My years truly belonged to him, and I had wholeheartedly acknowledged the fact. But I found I was still the administrator of them. Since they came to me one at a time, indeed one day at a time, I could only pay my debt in small installments. Jesus understood this when he said, "If anyone would come after me, he must deny himself and take up his cross daily and follow me" (Lk 9:23). And this meant that the impulsive choice of a moment on a hot August night had to become the choice of every moment that followed—

two of those choices I have already described.

Happily, Christ wanted to set me free even more than I wanted to be set free. And though, like everyone around me, I failed all too often to pay him what I owed, he pursued me relentlessly, teaching me in the thousands of small choices that I made how freedom could be found.

"So if the Son sets you free, you will be free indeed," Jesus once stated (Jn 8:36). Is there any difference between the kind of freedom Jesus gives and the freedom the young Communist seemed to experience in Mexico City? Do they share the same essential qualities? Both, after all, consist of being set free from petty enslavements to one great enslavement—an enslavement that liberates because I am doing what I want to do.

Let me say one more important thing about freedom: Freedom does not consist in doing what I want to do but in doing what I was designed to do. If I do what I want to do, I wind up not liking what I do. What at first promises liberty turns out to be a more onerous slavery.

You fling yourself with wild abandon to serve an ideology, and at first it feels like the most heady liberty you have ever known. But the high subsides. The sense of liberty goes. In the end, the grim, dreary enslavement seems no better than the enslavement to your former selfish whims.

It matters little whether the ideology is Communist or Christian. Many Christians find themselves enslaved to a hideous mixture of dogma, spiritual cliché and psychological technique. They are chained to a semi-Christian ideology rather than to a Person.

Do not misunderstand me. I do not underestimate the importance of truth. It is just that humanity was not designed to serve a theory—even a true theory. Theories enslave.

The truth is a Person. Jesus alone gives freedom to human

beings. He knows what he designed our beings for. He knows where true freedom exists for us. And he has infinite patience in teaching us, lesson by lesson, how to be free.

"Come to me," he invites us, "all you who are weary and burdened, and I will give you rest. Take my yoke upon you and learn from me, for I am gentle and humble in heart, and you will find rest for your souls. For my yoke is easy and my burden is light" (Mt 11:28-30).

Questions for Individuals or Groups

1. When has commitment meant following Christ's sacrificial example for you personally?

2. On pages 24-26 the author describes his experience of looking into Christ's eyes. When has the power of Christ's death moved you?

3. Do you know people who believe that "the more you suffer, the more spiritual your brand of Christianity is" (p. 26)? Describe them. How is this attitude a distortion of the truth?

4. How has dependence on your own works, rather than on God's grace, caused you to stumble in the past? How were you able to work through this?

5. How do you react to the author's statement, "Many devoted Christians for one reason or another have regarded all artistic expression as suspect except the composition of 'Christian' music, hymnwriting and the writing of Christian novels and such" (p. 28)? How do you think Christians can use their creativity to God's glory?

6. Describe the difference between lust and pleasure (p. 28).

7. When has concern for the (comparably) trivial details of your life distracted you from the gifts God was offering you (p. 35)?

8. Have you ever known a Christian who appeared as crazy as the man with the giant pearl in Matthew 13:45 (pp. 31-32)? How does this story change your perception of such a person?

9. Have you ever had to make a choice to give up something as the author did with his Victorian novels (p. 33)? Explain.

10. What attitudes are there to respect and embrace in the letter from the young communist (pp. 34-35)?

11. What does carrying the cross mean for you in your daily life?

12. Would you say that our society's values enslave people or free them? Explain. What enslaves Christians? How does enslavement to God mean that we are freed?

3

Pilgrim,
Stranger,
Displaced Person

Commitment to Christ always involves a radical change of citizenship. We have dual citizenship, involving a shift in loyalty, so that our prime attachment is to heaven, rather than earth. As committed Christians, we learn in time to think of heaven as *home* while our country of birth becomes a country in which we are aliens. We collaborate with Christ in furthering his purposes in that country.

No treachery is involved. Christ is the rightful ruler of every country, and obedience to him will in fact make us better citizens than we would otherwise be. We will respect its laws. In many countries we will find that basic law is molded to a considerable degree by Judeo-Christian thought. But in all countries at certain points in history, true Christians have found themselves uncomfortable in the country of their birth and have had to choose between obedience to God or to the State.

I choose the word *comfort* with care. Let me forget about heavenly citizenship for a moment and talk about our earthly countries of origin. I was born in Britain and lived a good deal of my early life there, but I visited France, Switzerland, the United States, the Caribbean, Egypt, India and Ceylon. However, I never spent long periods elsewhere and always thought of Britain as "home."

I was fascinated by the countries I visited, writing long letters home about them. I even envied many features of those countries—scenery, way of life, climate (Britain's climate is pathetic). But I would not have chosen to live elsewhere. Britain was home.

Later I spent a longer period in the States, married a Canadian there, and proceeded to spent ten years in various Latin American countries. We settled in Canada after that; though I continued to travel extensively, Canada became more like home, and our children did most of their growing up there.

It is now thirty-five years since I left Britain. I have been back for visits from time to time, but with each visit I noticed that Britain was no longer *my* Britain, no longer the Britain I knew as a boy and as a young man. At times the realization was painful. Cities and their streets changed, sometimes radically and totally. Landmarks disappeared. People I knew died or seemed to have grown old when I hadn't expected them to. There was a sort of Rip van Winkle effect after a time, a bewilderment and terrible sense of loss. And of course I had changed too.

The result is that I do not feel totally at home anywhere. You have to be born somewhere to be totally at home there. But you have to spend most of your life there too. I had broken the rule. So now, though I feel more at home in Canada than anywhere else in the world, I don't feel completely

at home even there. I talk wrong. I have little bits of British-
ness about me that I'll never shed and that will never allow
for total assimilation, even in Canada.

But notice the rule. To be completely at home you must be
born in a country *and spend most of your life there.* Immigrants
may say they are totally at home in the country of their
adoption, but I think that in many cases they are kidding
themselves a little. It is one thing to be a stranger in the
country of your birth, but quite another to be as much at
home in your country of adoption as the natives.

A Christian is someone who has been "born from above"—
that is, born a citizen of heaven. As Christians read Scripture,
the atmosphere of heaven and the culture of the celestial city
invades their being. As they meditate, as they pray, as they
spend time waiting in silence on God, the same thing begins
to happen at an accelerating pace. When they meet and worship with like-minded citizens of heaven, they are really
spending time in the country of their new birth. The degree
to which they feel at home in the celestial city depends upon
the amount of time they spend breathing its air, walking as
Enoch did—with God.

Abraham: Nomad or Displaced Person?

It would be a mistake to call Abraham a nomad. True, he
adopted a nomadic lifestyle. But the difference between Abraham and neighboring tribesmen was that, though Abraham
had left a settled existence behind, he was looking ahead, as
the committed Christian is, to a more permanent one. He was
in search of a country where he and his descendants could live
in peace.

Abraham never saw his vision turn into reality. Though he
found the country he was looking for, he never possessed it.
There is a sense in which we possess heaven now, for it is

"within us." But in a deeper sense we look for a country that still awaits us. As for Abraham, he remained a wandering stranger in the country he had intended to settle. He is described variously as pilgrim, sojourner and stranger. Were he a child of the twentieth century, we might call him a refugee or a displaced person.

Abraham is thus the prototype of the follower of Jesus. We do not live in tents as Abraham the sojourner did. We may not even be called to live out of a suitcase as some of our modern brothers and sisters are. Yet, if we are serious about following Christ, we share Abraham's outlook.

We do not belong. We are temporary residents only. Our real home is not immediately available, but we refuse to settle permanently anywhere else. We are pilgrims and strangers.

We have not chosen impermanence as a preferred lifestyle. We are not nomadic. A nomad thinks only of the next temporary pasture. Deep within us is a longing for our true home. It is this longing that characterizes the people of God. They do not belong to this world because they belong somewhere else.

Nor do they long for home because they want to escape from difficult circumstances. Such a longing would be pathological and escapist. The escapist is at home nowhere. Just as the nomad is thinking of the next pasture, so the escapist is always fleeing the previous one.

The urge to find a home is a deep human instinct. Something of its pathos and beauty has been seen during our century in the return of the descendants of Abraham to the earthly home of their forebears. The passion, the pain, the sufferings and the struggle, however ugly they may be in themselves, testify to the tenacity of the homing instinct.

If we judge by the people who are in modern Israel, we can make a generalization. People from areas of persecution feel the urge more keenly than people who are prosperous, settled and comfortable. Thus U.S. Jews may underwrite much of the financing that floats Israel, but U.S. Jews are much less likely to tear up their roots and move there than are Jews who are persecuted for being Jewish. A New York Jew and a Tel Aviv Jew are two very different people.

There is a parallel in the church. Christians who are prosperous and comfortable on earth may give money generously to Christian work but usually find it hard to think of heaven as home. It is one thing to speak piously about dying as going home, but quite another to deliberately put ourselves in life-threatening danger. Tragically, many who talk piously about "home" display little evidence of longing to be there. Home in Florida is more attractive. Tension exists between home on earth and home in heaven, and there are practical ways in which we can discover where our real interest lies.

Where Your Treasure Is

Psychoanalysts talk about *cathexis*. Cathexis means (approximately) emotional investment. To cathect something heavily means that your emotional life is pretty tangled up with whatever you cathect. The question that faces every Christian is this: Given that we are less concerned about heaven the more we are wrapped up with earth, and given that the more wrapped up in heaven we are, the less anxious we will be about our earthly home—how much cathexis do we invest in mansions in the skies? I grow weary of the cliché that describes some people as so heavenly minded that they are no earthly good. Years have passed since I met anyone fitting that description. By and large my Christian acquaintances are too earthly minded to be any heavenly good. And this should concern us far more.

Some years ago we were planning to make a move to another country. Our plan affected our outlook and behavior. It influenced our feelings about the house we lived in. We looked at our house through the eyes of a prospective buyer and were no longer concerned about making it more comfortable for ourselves. The move affected our buying habits. We stopped looking for good buys on winter clothes because there was no winter season where we were going. I weathered a Manitoba winter in a thin cheap winter coat. We found ourselves making do with gadgets that were wearing out rather than buying new ones. We put up with many minor inconveniences.

We were not being virtuous. We wanted to make sure we had money enough to make a good start in the country we were going to. We were reducing our cathexis in Canada and increasing it in the Caribbean. Our interest in Canada was diminishing while our interest in the Caribbean was growing.

Jesus was talking about exactly the same thing when he urged us to lay up treasure in heaven. His words blast our self-deception away: "For where your treasure is, there will your heart be also" (Mt 6:21)—a simple way to say that his followers would cathect heaven more than earth.

Jesus knew the tug of war in our hearts between heavenly and earthly homes. He knew our struggle between love of money and heavenly treasure. He told us we needed a "single" eye. He warned that without that single (or sound) eye, we would grope in terrible inner darkness (Mt 6:22-23 KJV). Torn perpetually in two directions, we could never see clearly the issues confronting us. We would go through life confused and bewildered, plagued with a sense of guilt and alienation, and never sure where we were going.

It is far easier for those who makes up their minds to pursue money and money alone. At least they know where they are going. Provided they are not hampered by qualms of conscience or the pull of other aims and ideals, they too will have a single eye. They cut a less pathetic figure than the Christian who straddles the fence.

It would be simpler if all Christians were called to vows of poverty. If we knew it was God's will that none of us own cars, or that all of us were allowed precisely two sets of underwear, one set of outerwear, one pair of slippers, one pair of shoes and fifty dollars a month in rent, we would all know where we stood.

But Jesus does not make it that easy. His teaching about giving away a second set of clothing to someone who has none is not an attempt to set maximum living standards. As a matter of fact, as any welfare officer knows, once we get into the realm of what we're entitled to and what we're not entitled to, we find many gray areas. More than that, instead of being focused on heaven, we do in fact become more thing-centered than ever. For instance, what do I do with my fifty dollar rent allowance when the choice lies between an inconvenient hovel ten miles from work at twenty-five dollars a month and a room nearby which is fifty-two dollars a month? Voluntary poverty has many subtle problems, and it can still leave a person a secret worshiper of mammon.

No One Can Serve Two Masters

Jesus wanted to set us free from mammon in our hearts. The following illustration makes this abundantly clear. "No one can serve two masters. . . ." he states categorically. "You cannot serve both God and Money" (Mt 6:24). Mammon or money, in the context, seems to refer to care about material necessities. He is concerned, as he always is, with the inner struggle we all experience between things and God.

Quite often we speak of the rat race. Rats may well enjoy (we have no means of knowing) the exercise wheels that accompany their cages. But to humans, the wheel symbolizes the endless struggle of daily living with its depressing sense of never moving forward. It is difficult to avoid getting trapped in a rat race if one lives in the Western world. We are gripped by the delusion that if we earn a little more money, we will be set free. But the carrot of better and finer toys dangles perpetually before our noses, so that we spend more than we earn. To their horror, a couple discovers that they are making $100,000 annually but that the goal of freedom is still another $20,000 or $30,000 away. Like a mirage in the desert, the goal has receded from them as they advanced.

Another person may earn $150,000 and feel the bitterness of slavery in his or her soul. You may say, "If I earned that much, I wouldn't feel enslaved," and proceed to tell me how you would go about freeing up your time. But if you are not free now with the income you earn, you will be no more free with fifty times as much. Freedom is an inner contentment with what you have. It means to covet only heavenly treasure.

Such an attitude frees us not only because we feel free psychologically, but because it frees our vision. It enables us to look at life in a new way, so that we may discover, for instance, that we do not need to work the long hours we do but could spend more hours in direct involvement with building the kingdom.

We may now begin to see why Jesus did not concentrate on precisely what possessions a person should have, but rather on our need to decide between God and mammon. For the decision against mammon is a decision to say: "I am here only a little while. All I need is enough to keep myself and my dependents alive. If God should give me more (and he is a very bountiful God), I shall accept gladly what he provides. But I shall not pursue it or make myself a slave for more than

I actually need. My real treasure is in heaven."

I can hear in my mind a background of voices using words like "practical, realistic and sense of proportion or responsibility." I am sure their unending chorus will continue till the close of time. Even when I am questioned about definitions ("How do you define the amount you need to stay alive? Are you talking about just keeping body and soul together or are things like health and education necessary?" and so forth), I refuse to rise to the bait. Once we get into definitions of that kind, we shall slowly become fascinated with the here and now. Things like *need* define themselves once our priorities are straightened out. *Need* at one point in time and space is not the same as in another. But who cares? What we are talking about is freedom from ambivalence, not about how many hairs make a beard.

Our Treasure in Heaven

I cannot leave this whole question, however, without discussing treasure in heaven. I have already confessed that I don't know what the treasure is. Obviously it is valuable to us hereafter. Just as obviously, it will not cause us the anxiety earthly investments do (Mt 6:19-20). Securities belie their name. Banks and insurance companies will pass away. Precious metals have all through history been stolen. There is no such thing on earth as a safe investment—not even a fairly safe one. But heavenly treasure is guaranteed by the name of Jehovah. It is of value. It is secure.

Yet how little importance we attach to it.

You see, to store up heavenly treasure takes earthly time— time that otherwise could be devoted to pursuing cars and carpets. This is the whole point in what Jesus is saying. And we reveal where our interest lies by the way we distribute our energies. Just as Roman Catholics in past years sought to buy heavenly favors with earthly cash, so evangelicals try to buy heavenly treasure by giving money to missions. We cannot buy heavenly treasure with dollars. The exchange rate is zilch. We have to labor for heavenly treasure just as we would for earthly rewards. The only difference is that the one labor is a joy and a delight while the other enslaves.

What exactly is the treasure? Scripture never says. In the parables, faithful stewards get to reign. The explicit teaching of Paul is, "If we endure [suffer with him], we will also reign with him" (2 Tim 2:12). Are the rewards of reigning and the treasure one and the same? Perhaps yes; perhaps no.

It is interesting to notice how different treasures affect people. Pearls, diamonds and gold are associated with piracy, theft, murder, holdups, anxiety, greed, cruelty, torture. The longing to possess them awakens unwholesome passions in humanity. What if, as many commentators suggest, the treasure were an increased capacity to appreciate Christ? Certainly a longing to know Christ in all his beauty has a very different effect on Christians than the chance of making a million dollars.

Living the Examined Life
Look at yourself in the mirror of Christ's word. Ask the person you see in the mirror: "Where is my treasure? Where is my heart? Where do my real ambitions lie? Am I a child of the country my body was born in—or a true hybrid—someone who is also a citizen of eternity?" Look hard at your mirror image. Do not evade the eyes you see. They will tell you the truth; and you need to face the truth if you are to be freed. Deep in your heart you want to be set free, but you must look first at your chains:

Our souls are held by what they hold;
Slaves still are slaves in chains of gold;

To whatsoever we may cling,
We make it a soul-chaining thing;
Whether it be a life, or land,
And dear as our right eye or hand.[3]

Struggle in your chains to Jesus. Ask him to break them for
you. Then pick them up and fling them into the eternal fires.
Declare before the unseen host of onlookers, "I am a citizen
of heaven. I have one Lord and him only will I serve." As you
do so you will experience what Charles Wesley describes:

My chains fell off
My heart was free,
I rose, went forth
And followed Thee.[4]

How then do we labor for treasure in heaven? The theme
recurs in the gospels in both parables and in Jesus' teaching.

Two ideas seem paramount. One is that we have been
given certain potential (time, opportunities, abilities and so
forth) which can be employed in the interest of the kingdom.
Each of us is responsible to God to render to him from the
potential that he has given us. The second and related idea
is that, according to how well we use the potential, we will
be given reward or treasure.

I have already pointed out that it is possible for many of us
to free our time to serve God once we get our priorities
sorted out. I know an insurance agent, for instance, who
gives his summer months to Christian camps and lives on his
winter earnings. Anyone who is his own boss can figure out
a similar plan.

I am not saying that earning money is secular and that
Christian camps constitute "true Christian service." Rather,
I am saying that many of us would find we had more time
than we thought if we made money less of a priority.

What is your own potential? What has God given you in

time, in money, in physique, in natural gifts and in spiritual abilities? In what way can they be used for the kingdom, and to what extent have you used this potential?

Have you used it at all today? This week? This past month? As you look back over the year, to what extent have you been living for God?

If your conscience troubles you, how soon can you act? When you complete your education? When you get another job? When you get married?

Could you start now?

Questions for Individuals and Groups

1. The author describes the many places he has lived. To what extent can you identify with his experience of being a foreigner? Explain. What kinds of feelings do you think Abraham would have had as a nomad?

2. Describe a situation when you didn't feel as though you quite belonged. What is the difference between healthy tension with the world and escapism (p. 44)?

3. What does it mean to be "too earthly minded to be any heavenly good" (p. 45)? What are the things which cause you to be earthly minded?

4. How can we be set free from the power of money? How much money do you think you need? How has this goal changed throughout your life?

5. What do you think heavenly treasure is (p. 50)?

6. What are the keys to seeking for this heavenly treasure and rejecting earthly treasure (p. 51)? What kinds of choices does this mean for you personally?

7. How are you using your gifts to build the kingdom right now?

4

The Loyalty
That Calls
for Hatred

We have seen that the committed life is the life that has chosen the way of the cross. We have also seen that though such a life may include suffering and pain, it is a full and joyous life. But what happens to your relationship with other people when you commit your life to Christ in this way?

When we were children, being friends with some kids meant being the enemies of others. We made changes according to who was more important to us. So it is with Christ. When we opt for him, we make very powerful friends and real enemies. But the matter is by no means simple, especially as it affects the members of our own families.

If we commit ourselves to Jesus Christ, we automatically change every other relationship in our lives. When he becomes supreme to us, other people slip into different places. Those nearest us may become alienated. Those whom we once abhorred will become dear and intimate. The question of future marriage assumes a new solemnity. The re-evaluation and reorientation that follow commitment apply not only to values, but also to people.

The Paradox of Love and Hate

"Whoever acknowledges me before men," Jesus tells us, "I will also acknowledge him before my Father in heaven. But whoever disowns me before men, I will disown him before my Father in heaven. Do not suppose that I have come to bring peace to the earth. I did not come to bring peace, but a sword. For I have come to turn 'a man against his father, and a daughter against her mother, and a daughter-in-law against her mother-in-law—a man's enemies will be the members of his own household.' Anyone who loves his father or mother more than me is not worthy of me; and anyone who loves his son or daughter more than me is not worthy of me; and anyone who does not take his cross and follow me is not worthy of me. Whoever finds his life will lose it, and whoever loses his life for my sake will find it" (Mt 10:32-39).

But on another occasion he said, "Why do you break the command of God for the sake of your tradition? For God said, 'Honor your father and mother,' and, 'Anyone who curses his father or mother must be put to death.' But you say that if a man says to his father or mother, 'Whatever help you might otherwise have received from me is a gift devoted to God,' [For example, we might say, "I have given to Christian work the support I used to give to you"], he is not to 'honor his father' with it. Thus you nullify the word of God for the sake of your tradition" (Mt 15:3-6).

When we examine the words of Jesus, we discover paradoxes which at first seem confusing and contradictory. We are told to honor and respect our parents. Jesus vigorously condemns making God's work an excuse for ignoring parents' financial needs. Yet he also tells us that if we follow him we must "hate" those nearest to us (Lk 14:25-26). What does his teaching mean? Is it consistent?

Before we try to answer these questions, let us notice that the Bible is just as confusing about other relationships. Friendships can be dangerous. The godly man does not walk in the counsel of the ungodly; he does not stand in the way of sinners (Ps 1:1). Repeatedly, we are warned against friendship with evildoers. Yet in strange contrast we find Jesus himself eating with tax gatherers, prostitutes and sinners. As a physician seeks out the sick, so the Savior sought out sinners. And he urged his followers to do the same.

How do we explain the apparent contradiction? Does the Christian, perhaps, never truly befriend a non-Christian, but approach him as a fisherman lures a fish or a salesman a likely prospect? The idea is abhorrent to most of us. Would Jesus, the great Fisher of Men, regard sinners with so calculating an eye? Does he not rather, like the Good Samaritan, feel his heart moved with compassion?

The difficulty begins to resolve itself when we realize that there are two elements in our feelings for someone else. I want my friends to like me, and I also want to show kindness to them; there is my longing that they will understand me and there is my concern to understand them. Both elements—the need element and the giving element—are present in any relationship, but they show themselves in different ways and may exist in different proportions.

Jim, an immature husband of forty, weeps bitterly when his wife walks out. He admits he has been a poor husband, yet says: "But God knows I love her. I can't live without her." As we talk, it becomes evident that he is still highly critical of his wife. A stream of bitter words pour through his lips as he describes the woman he says he loves. "She has no heart. She can't leave! How can she do this to me? She's mean. She has no feelings."

"I love her. She has no heart." What is he saying? He's telling me that he wants this woman to be nice to him—to come back, hold his hand, darn his socks, make his meals and go to bed with him. He has the same kind of feeling for her as he had for his momma and his teddy bear.

But he has no compassion for her. He does not grieve over the pain she endures. He has little concern for her happiness, only for his own.

How different were the feelings of the father of the prodigal son (Lk 15:11-32). Knowing full well the difficulties and dangers his son faced, he still gave him his part of the legacy and let him leave home, concealing his own aching heart. The old man must have watched daily from the housetop, straining his aging eyes, yearning for his own flesh and blood. But he had let the boy go. Therefore, he must also have perceived the needs and longings in the boy's own heart and suppressed his personal yearnings for the sake of his son.

We can now understand the apparent contradictions in the passages we examined. For there are differing elements at work in our relationships.

Joe, an insecure adolescent from a fundamentalist home, yearns for the approval and admiration of his peers. If they smoke, he must smoke more. If they have sex (or say they do), his stories of conquest must outrank theirs.

When his letters to his girlfriends fell into his parents' hands, they found themselves shaking and weak in response to the appalling obscenity and evil they read. Yet these are his friends, he protested. They understand him. They're his buddies. Sure, he shouldn't have said those things. He was mostly bragging anyway. It's not that big a deal. But his friends—he can't give up his friends.

Why? Because he needs to feel wanted and accepted, and at last he has found a group that admires him. His parents asked, "Do you talk to them of Christ?"

He hung his head. "Well, they know you guys are religious. I told them I have to go to church. But they don't mind. They're pretty decent about it."

At this point friendship with the world is indeed enmity with God. For Joe's actions are based on his pathetic need to be accepted and admired. To get what he wants, he is willing to pay too high a price. Much as we may sympathize, we know he is selling his birthright too cheaply. Millions of men and women have abandoned the treasures of heaven and run downhill with the crowd for the same pitiable reason. Friendship with evildoers under these circumstances is wrong and harmful.

All of us share Joe's problem in some degree. It affects our relationships with those closest to us.

How does the Muslim convert feel when he is hounded from home and village because he confessed Christ? He need only retract his confession. He could even keep it secret—and the family would welcome him into its bosom again. No, he is not hating them as he is driven from their midst. But a new love, greater than any love he has ever before experienced, so grips his heart that even love of family can be called hate in comparison with that love. Yet he weeps as he goes and his heart is heavy.

And what do you do when family and friends mock you?

Once again, Jesus never permits us to fail in our responsibilities. He insists we give love and affection to our parents, spouses, children and anyone else who may have a claim on us. Even money given to God's work, when it is given at the expense of our needy relatives, is a sin against God's holy law

(Mt 15:3-6). The apostle Paul calls someone who fails to provide for his family "worse than an infidel" (1 Tim 5:8 KJV). On the cross Jesus was still concerned about the welfare of the mother he left behind.

Family, especially a warm and happy family, comforts and cherishes its members. To hate one's family means to be so committed to Christ that, however much it costs me to be away from that circle, I must cut myself ruthlessly from its comfort and follow him barefoot on rocky pathways. It means that when my wife and I are parted, we must embrace and say, "It won't be long. It's for Jesus' sake."

Paradox and a Premonition
Hate?

Once I had a premonition that my wife and infant son would be killed in a flying accident. We were to travel separately from the U.S. to Bolivia, South America. She would fly via Brazil and Buenos Aires, then north to Bolivia. I was to visit Mexico, several Central American countries, Venezuela, Colombia and other countries to strengthen Christian work among students, before joining my family in Bolivia.

The premonition came with sickening certainty just before we parted on the night of a wild snowstorm. I felt I was a cowardly fool as I drove away and saw Lorrie silhouetted in the yellow light of the doorway, surrounded by swirling snowflakes. Why didn't I go back and tell her I would cancel the flights? Why didn't I act on this foreboding?

I didn't believe in premonitions—and had never even heard of "words of knowledge." Lorrie would probably laugh. Besides I was late, I had to get to the place where I would spend the night before my early morning flight. No conversation was possible with the man who was driving me to my hotel. Fear, shame, guilt and nausea all boiled inside me.

In bed I tossed in misery. Of course I prayed. By faith I was going to have it licked. Faith? In the presence of so powerful a premonition? My mouth was dry. My limbs shook. God was a million miles away. The hours crawled by, each one a year of fear. Why didn't I get dressed, hire a car and go back to them?

"What's the matter? Can't you trust me?"

I was startled. Was God speaking?

"Yes, I'll trust you—if you promise to give them back to me."

Silence.

Then, "And if I don't promise? If I don't give them back to you, will you stop trusting me?"

"Oh, God, what are you saying?" My heart had stopped and I couldn't breathe.

"Can you not entrust them to me in death as well as in life?"

Suddenly a physical warmth flowed through all my body. I think I wept a little. My words came tremblingly and weakly, "Yes, I place them in your hands. I know you will take care of them in life or in death."

And my trembling subsided. Peace—better by far than martinis on an empty stomach—flowed over and over me. And drowsily I drifted off to sleep.

Hate them? How could I ever hate them? Yet by faith I had said in effect, I will do your will whatever it costs to me or them, and I will trust you.

Their plane crashed. Everyone on board was killed. But my wife had also had a premonition and cut their journey short, getting off the plane the stop before the tragedy occurred.

I am grateful for the way it worked out. But I didn't know beforehand that things would go as they did. And had it not worked out that way, I would have grieved (God knows how

I would have grieved), but I would not have regretted my decision to trust and to go forward.

But the issue affects friends as well as family members. It affects Christian brothers and sisters. Recently, I have been studying the history of revivals, only to find that far from being times of heaven on earth, they have commonly proved to be times when two things seem to be happening simultaneously. First, God's spirit is being poured out, sinners are being convicted and converted, saints are being renewed and refreshed, and the church is advancing. But at the same time hostility, bitterness and name-calling among Christians is reaching an unprecedented climax. Not all Christians understand what is happening. Many are threatened by what God is doing. Some see it as a threat to "their" work. And there are usually genuinely godly people on both sides.

Jonathan Edwards, George Whitefield, John Wesley in their day, and Moody in his, all felt the keen winds of Christian hatred cut through to their hearts. Rejection is doubly painful when it comes from people we respect, and it is often the case that Christian leaders are the first to criticize those whom God uses in a new way. Jesus said it would be so and it remains so to this day. We whiten the gravestones of the saintly heroes of the past till they gleam. But our Christian forebears punished on a pillory, and in some cases killed, those same saintly heroes. And on a smaller scale the same fate awaits any Christian who takes commitment to Christ seriously.

At this point the issue of persecution arises from either the household of God or from non-Christians—and even from the state. I will deal with the broader issues of persecution later, particularly the matter of persecution by the state. In this chapter we are focusing on the more immediate matter of changing relationships, and in particular about what Christ was talking about when he told us to hate people for his sake. *Hate* may create the wrong picture in our minds. From a broad understanding of his own teaching we see that he is telling us to love and follow him *even though it means we could be misunderstood, rejected or even persecuted by those whose friendship and support are precious to us.*

Both pain and doubt can arise when this happens. In the shock of being misunderstood and even rejected, how do we react? Equally important, if following Christ can sometimes mean encountering even Christian opposition, how can we be sure that we are not mistaken in the way we are going?

The two problems are linked. If pain should force us to ask ourselves whether we have mistaken the path, then for that reason alone pain is a good thing. If we are to face misunderstanding and rejection, we must be sure of what we are doing, for godly certainty itself reduces pain. But where does certainty come from?

Certainty comes from the character of God. Christ reveals that character to be of utter faithfulness. Christ never forsakes his followers. If in humble trust you commit yourself to him, he will not let you get very far astray. You may make mistakes, but he will correct you before very long. His Spirit will convict you, either through the ongoing illumination of Scripture or through help from other sources. So look back at the step which brought the trouble on. Ask him, "Did you really tell me to do that?" or "Is that really what your Word means?"

But let me approach this as a psychiatrist. We all wear glasses when we read Scripture—or when we consider any truth or supposed truth. They are spectacles made up of our hidden psychological needs and weaknesses—for always the greatest obstacle to our understanding lies hidden deep within our own hearts. Our first prayer then must be that God will make us aware of the spectacles resting on our noses, that is, of the secret motivations of our hearts.

Some of us may have a need to assert our independence, to demonstrate that we are right. Others of us will be hungering for human approval. We will always have a tendency to opt for the "truth" which ministers to our deepest psychological need. Pray therefore that God will show you the motivation of your own heart—that is, the spectacles you are wearing. Is it your need to be liked and understood? Your pride and insecurity? Or a mixture of things?

For instance, when we are criticized by old friends but applauded by new, some of us will yearn to be understood and approved of, preferably by both groups. Our need for approval (from either group) can prevent us from seeing the truth. Our goal in life must never be popularity. Remember the words of Jesus, "Woe to you when all men speak well of you, for that is how their fathers treated the false prophets" (Lk 6:26).

It is important that we bring ourselves before God. He alone must search us. To indulge in an orgy of self-recrimination is neither healthy nor wise. Satan the Accuser is always ready to load us with false guilt. When the Holy Spirit points out the secrets of our hearts, his object is always to set us free and to draw us closer to himself. We may need to humble ourselves before him. Our psychological weaknesses always result in sinful heart attitudes, which must be confessed—as sin. But the net result will always be a freeing and a strengthening. It will result in joy and greater depth of conviction— whether of the rightness of our original course, or else of some mistaken understanding of what commitment to Christ really means.

The need for human approval is the most critical issue of all. It spells the difference between a soldier of Christ and a wimp. Unfortunately, we live in a society governed by *image*. Commercial enterprises spend millions on developing their public images. Lumber companies may rape the land for decades, stripping mountainsides and exposing the land to erosion and animal species to extinction, while sponsoring TV commercials emphasizing the importance of reforestation and featuring their belated tokenism in research and tree planting. It is the image the public has that matters.

It is the same in politics. Presidents and presidential candidates employ image burnishers. Impression matters. Image makes for a smoother road to position and power. A recent *Time* essay by Michael Kinsley entitled, "Thatcher for President" makes the point plain. Kinsley is a liberal. It was not Mrs. Thatcher's political philosophy that mattered to him so much as her courage and her contempt for the politics of image. He asserts that Thatcher is a leader, whereas "Reagan was not, nor is Bush." Kinsley goes on to write,

Even after ten years and three election victories, Margaret Thatcher is not a beloved or even an especially liked figure in Britain. She never has been. And yet—despite a midterm slump in the polls—she would probably win a fourth term election tomorrow. . . . surely even the coddled and petted American voter could respond to a politician who did not go a-whoring after popularity, who offered spinach instead of candy and who asked for respect instead of love. Such a politician would not have to be a conservative—or even a woman."[5]

Unhappily, the church is influenced far too much by the need to polish her image. Church leaders are by no means free from the politics of image. All of us who make up the church are more concerned than we should be about what everyone thinks about us. The lust for popularity corrupts us all.

True leaders defy unpopularity. They do what they believe

to be right come storm or sun. Real commitment to Christ will make us leaders, but will not necessarily make us popular. It will call for us to walk along the way of the cross.

And while it is one thing to be reassured that we are on track, that we are not succumbing to the need to be liked, it is quite another to deal with the pain of rejection. We may, as God has searched our hearts, already have chosen to sacrifice the praise of others for the praise of God. But the pain of being misunderstood by those we love will still be there. And it will take time to go away.

I know of no greater test of Christian maturity than the capacity genuinely to love those who criticize and reject us. Whatever happens, we must not give way to bitterness and resentment. Being cursed, we bless. We recognize that behind their rejection, our former friends have problems of their own. Our real enemy is the one who stirs up strife among brethren. Our brush with rejection must be viewed as an opportunity for vital spiritual growth. Having seen how sensitive we are, we hand our weakness to the Lord and sternly deal with our negative attitudes.

This is what it means to follow Christ fully. This is the effect he wants to have on all our personal relationships— family members, spouses, friends—whatever they may be. The fear that may hold you back is a fear of unbelief. But defy your fear and go forward. For to follow Christ fully means to take steps along the perilous pathway of trust, roped to the safest Guide in the universe.

Questions for Individuals and Groups

1. When you first made a commitment to Christ, did it change any of your relationships with others? What continuing effect has your commitment to Christ had on the significant relationships in your life?

2. Have you ever been in a friendship with someone who pulled you away from following Christ? How did you resolve this?

3. Have you ever had relationships with non-Christians which were glorifying to God? How were you able to be a positive influence without being negatively influenced?

4. How do you react to the author's experience of a premonition that the plane his wife and son were on would crash (pp. 58-59)? When have you trusted God to that extent? Explain.

5. Many Christians have been rejected by their friends and family because of their relationship with Christ. How do you feel when you realize that Christ will never forsake you?

6. When have you sought popularity and affirmation from friends, rather than seeking to serve Christ?

7. How do you deal with rejection from your friends? Why do you think they react negatively to you?

5

Suffering and the Christian

All along I have emphasized that the rewards of commitment and the way of the cross far outweigh its pains. But it must be apparent by now that pain is involved. Perhaps it is time to face the issue of suffering head on. Why should there be any suffering in the world? Why in particular should Christians suffer? What attitude ought we to adopt to our own suffering and to that of others?

For years I felt guilty because I never seemed to be committed deeply enough to Christ. However much I gave up I knew I could always have given up more. My life seemed as far removed from the book of Acts as from Elisabeth Elliot's *Through Gates of Splendor*. I could not get to the kernel of Christian commitment, so my Christian life was haunted by guilt. But the guilt was not true guilt. I was, I suppose, being taunted by the Accuser. The false sense of guilt arose because I did not understand what real commitment was all about.

One problem in particular troubled me. I had the feeling that I should be suffering more, doing without more. Yet when I did suffer, it sometimes seemed to arise from my lack of commitment and at other times bore no relation whatever to it.

The cost of commitment is the price we pay for following the way of the cross. But you, like me, may suffer many things which have nothing to do with commitment. I must therefore begin by excluding other forms of suffering that Christians encounter.

The Common Lot of Humanity

Philip Yancey once quoted Helmut Thielicke as saying, "They [American Christians] have an inadequate theology of suffering." Yancey went on to ask, "How could we expect a theology of suffering to emerge from a society that has survived two centuries without a foreign invasion, solves all meteorological discomfort with 'climate control,' and prescribes a pill for every twinge of pain?" We are soft, resentful of pain, terrified of discomfort. We live in a society which sees comfort as a basic right. And as part of that society we have unwittingly shaped our theology of suffering accordingly.

Let my try to put Christian suffering in its proper context. We suffer, as all human beings suffer, *because we are part of a fallen humanity*. We live in a world of pain. Though we know joy and beauty, though we may throw back our heads and look awestruck at the night sky, yet there is pain. Though we are moved to happiness by the call of seagulls, the silent loveliness of coral reefs, clean smells after rainfall or the white sweep of a ski slope, yet there is pain. Though the touch of a grandchild's hand within our palm or the memory of a winter night by a glowing stove stir contentment in us, yet all of this is only half the story. The stove once burned our childish fingers. The grandchild walking beside us may have a father who abandoned the child and his mother for alcohol. Ski slopes and coral reefs delight the rich while millions starve. Beauty and goodness, anguish and horror come mingled to us.

God does not apologize for our suffering, although we may sneer at his omnipotence, his love or both. He has left us the scorching dignity of pain because he gave us real choices with real consequences. Inevitably, the consequences brought tragedy on the heads of others as well as on our own.

The woman whose child was kidnapped and murdered may not ask: Why did God take my baby? It was not God who killed her baby but evil humans. God weeps with her.

Yet if God weeps and is almighty, why does he not intervene?

I cannot in a few sentences explain the problem of evil. I could not explain it were I to write a whole book about the problem. God and his ways transcend my understanding. But I have a few ideas.

In the first place, there are things that even an omnipotent God cannot do. He cannot do them either because they are *by their very nature* impossible or else *because they violate his own integrity*. Things that are by their nature impossible are what C. S. Lewis calls "intrinsic impossibilities."

To say that God can create an object that is a perfectly spherical cube is not to extol his power but to talk nonsense. The words are meaningless, and as Lewis points out, to put "God can" in front of a nonsensical sentence does not turn it into sense.[6]

So, to give humanity freedom to choose and to act, and at the same time to deny them that freedom, is meaningless. If God gives us power to choose, then we may choose evil. And, reality being what it is, the evil can harm others.

Lewis describes this in an allegorical fantasy, in which "the Landlord" represents God, "the country" represents the world and the tenants represent human beings. The hero of the story, John, receives from his mentor an explanation of why the Landlord is helpless. The mentor explains that the Landlord has taken the risk of working the country with free tenants instead of slaves in chain gangs; and, as they are free, there is no way of making it impossible for them, to go into forbidden places and eat forbidden fruits. Up to a certain point he can work with them, even when they have done so, and break them of the habit. But beyond that point—you can see for yourself. People can go on eating mountain-apples so long that *nothing* will cure their craving for it: and the very worms it breeds inside them will make them more certain to eat more.

But the matter goes deeper. The universe in which we live, spoiled though it may be by humanity's sinful fall, still reflects God's own nature. It is consistent with his being. And God must be true to himself. He cannot and will not betray his own being. For instance, he cannot and will not lie. Nor can he break his covenants.

We may see no reason why he should not so control us that wars would cease. But to do so would make us subhuman and make nonsense of God's covenant with us. And even if God could do that (which he cannot), would any of us seriously want to be part of a race of benign humanoid computers, manipulated by an omnipotent Celestial Scientist? Robots like HAL, R2D2, C3PO and their more modern successors are intriguing in fiction, but who would want to become one of them? I am not a machine, and I would never wish to become one. It is neither my mental agility nor my skill in learning from experience that makes me human, nor even my ability to experience emotion. Rather it is my capacity to transcend earth's bounds and know the Creator who made me in his image, not as a slave but as a son. It is true that machines cannot suffer—yet what a price to pay to avoid suffering!

Such is the solution behaviorist B. F. Skinner in fact offered us. In *Walden II* and in *Beyond Human Dignity*, Skinner called for a world governed by behaviorist principles. Humans could be trained as dogs are trained, programmed as computers are programmed. He recognized that a human dignity is ignored when people are trained in the same way as circus animals. But Skinner felt that there are more important issues than the dignity of human beings. He wanted to go beyond human dignity.

The theory is folly. We must learn from history. Whenever rulers have forgotten the dignity of their human subjects, tyranny and oppression have followed. Indeed we could go further. Wherever in history there has been an emphasis on the idea that human beings reflect the nature and image of God himself, society has recognized the dignity of men, women and children, slavery has been reacted against, and suffering has been recognized as an evil to be eradicated.

But I must leave the unfathomable mystery of why suffering exists. If we cannot fathom God's wisdom, at least we can know his heart. His response to our plight was to live among us, drinking the dregs of our suffering that he might fill up a cup of salvation for us. Soon he will write the last chapter of our history and bring in his reign of peace.

For the present, the suffering goes on. And because we Christians are human, we share with humanity toothache and heartache, broken bones and fractured friendships, degenerative diseases and social decay. Just as the sun shines on both the just and unjust, so bacteria invade the bodies of both the sinner and saint.

We Christians also suffer *from our personal sins and stupidities.* When self-centeredness and pride wreck a Christian marriage, the pain is caused by sin. When a drug-crazed Christian teen-ager drives off an icy road at ninety miles an hour, he burns to death in his own flaming folly. If we are not immune from the common suffering of humanity, we can certainly demand no special protection from the consequences of our asinine self-will. We live in a world where fire burns. While guardian angels are a reality, there are no asbestos-robed saints.

Trained by Suffering

Again, Christians suffer *by way of discipline.* If we accept God's discipline with humble, believing hearts, our lives grow purer and our faith stronger. "Consider it pure joy, my brothers," writes James, "whenever you face trials of many kinds, because you know that the testing of your faith develops perseverance. Perseverance must finish its work so that you may be mature and complete, not lacking in anything" (Jas 1:2-4).

To grasp the secret of disciplinary suffering is to experience a transformation. Your bewilderment and dismay turn to joy. Strength makes resolute your enfeebled limbs and a song rises in your throat. "No discipline seems pleasant at the time, but painful" notes the writer to the Hebrews, "Later on, however, it produces a harvest of righteousness and peace for those who have been trained by it" (Heb 12:11).

For those who have been trained by it . . . Trained by suffering? How? And how do I know whether the suffering has come because of my own sin or because God is teaching me?

I may not always know. And in any case, the cause matters relatively little. What matters is my reaction to suffering. For I may be "trained by" suffering without understanding fully the reasons giving rise to it. To be trained by suffering I must have faith in God. He is still the active ruler of the universe. He is still my heavenly Father. He knows what I suffer and he cares.

For all of this I must thank and praise him. Moreover, in a way that defies analysis, God is able to bring good out of evil. He awaits only my confidence in him to turn suffering into a knife to carve away moral cancer. As drought in the summer makes tree roots dig deeper into the soil or as exhausting training increases the power and speed of an athlete, so suffering makes saints.

In suffering, then, I give thanks. I give thanks not *for* the suffering—God is not training me in masochism—but *in* it. I thank him that his grace is sufficient. I thank him that he is well able to deliver me and that in his own time he will. I thank him that he can turn the suffering to serve his own purposes in my life. I thank him that because Jesus, as a human, suffered more than I ever will, God understands how I feel from personal experience.

And as I praise and thank him, I become aware of two things. The suffering lessens. It lessens because peace in suffering halves its intensity, so that the anxiety and fear that accompanied it have gone. In addition, hope as well as a sense of *meaning* is born in the suffering. I become almost excited that it will turn to my good. No longer do I wonder how I can bear the suffering. Suffering becomes a sort of chariot on which I ride to new planes of living.

A passage from my book *The Fight* describes how God first brought this lesson home to me:

My oldest boy, Scott, was born badly crippled in Bolivia. For the first year of his life he was locked in what looked like brutal splints. (They caused him little or no suffering however.) When he was a year old the splints were removed, and soon he was running and walking. Inevitably he had his first fall, splitting his chin widely with a gash that extended up into the floor of his mouth.

We were far from civilization. I had no surgical instruments, only a pair of eyebrow tweezers and household needles and thread. I had no means of relieving pain. Firm hands gripped his tiny form as I inflicted what must have seemed like unbelievable pain on my terrified son. To say my heart was breaking sounds sentimental, yet his pain was my pain. Why was there no way I could comfort him with the knowledge that all would be well? I agonized over his ordeal as I gripped his tender skin with eyebrow tweezers and brutally jabbed a sewing needle again and again into his chin.[7]

Scott was in the same position we are when God teaches us something through suffering—with one difference. He could not understand. We can.

We have questions. Why is the pain necessary? The biblical answer is that it "produces a harvest of righteousness and peace for those who have been trained by it" (Heb 12:11). It is always aimed at correcting a specific weakness or fault in us. In Scott's case his injury could have become infected, and in that case could even have threatened his life. To sew the wound immediately made infection less likely. Again, to have left it open was to run the risk of an ugly scar on the lower part of his face. The scar is now unnoticeable. I was doing the best I could for him.

Why can't God explain things to us? Why can't he tell us what the specific weakness is? I suppose one answer is that he can; it is we who have a job hearing his voice. It is a problem in reception, not in transmission. You may say, "Why does he *have* to use pain—is there no other way?" Of course there is. There are many ways God has of changing us. He speaks to us in our circumstances, but as C. S. Lewis says, he *shouts* to us in our pain.[8]

But the pain is not a punishment. I was not punishing Scott as I inflicted such pain on him. Nor is God doing so with us. Instituting discipline, perhaps, but not punishment. And I knew from the agony that wrenched my whole body that God too suffers. When you discipline your own beloved child, you suffer with that child.

God suffers with you. If you grasp that, and if you can really trust him that *he knows what he is doing* and that you are in very competent hands, the pain will not go away entirely, but it will be reduced by half. As I have pointed out already, fear doubles pain. Trust halves it.

For Jesus' Sake

But in this book I am not talking about suffering we share with all humanity, nor suffering arising from our own stupidity and sin, nor yet disciplinary suffering. When I speak of Christian suffering, I am referring to that suffering I experience *because of my loyalty to Christ*. I do not mean suffering because of the way I witness (although some of us suffer because we are obnoxious and self-righteous in our attempts to evangelize) but suffering that arises because I stand close to the suffering Christ.

Christian suffering has to do with the cross I take up and heave on my back. It is suffering because of a deliberate choice. The kind of cross to which Christ refers is not a "cross" of rheumatism or of the petty annoyances that older evangelicals used to label their cross in life. It is the badge of a true follower of Jesus. It may take any form—sickness, hunger, loneliness, persecution, death. It has been the glory of the church for two thousand years. And to all who read this book, the words of the Lord of the church come ringing across the centuries: "Be faithful even to the point of death, and I will give you the crown of life" (Rev 2:10).

Questions for Individuals and Groups

1. On page 67 the author says he often felt guilty because he never seemed to be committed enough to the Christian life. What have been the ups and downs of your commitment since you've been a Christian? What were you able to identify as the real problem?

2. How do you react to the Philip Yancey quote on page 68 regarding the lack of an adequate theology of suffering in the United States? Do you think his assessment is accurate or inaccurate? Explain.

3. In your own words, how do you explain why God allows Christians to suffer?

4. Why, according to pages 69-71, does God give humanity the power to choose evil? How satisfying do you find this answer to be? Explain.

5. What does the author mean by the phrase "there are no asbestos-robed saints" (p. 72)?

6. When have you suffered due to your own fault? When have you felt that your suffering was a result of God disciplining you? How did you react in each case?

7. What is the difference between praising God *for* suffering and *in* suffering (p. 73)? How has praise been a part of your experience of suffering?

8. How does the author's story about his son help you to understand what God experiences when we suffer (pp. 73-75)? What does it mean to you in your suffering to know that God also suffers?

9. How is suffering because of Christ different from the general experience of suffering (p. 75)?

6

Jesus
and
Suffering

*L*et us address that particular kind of suffering which comes from being committed to following Jesus. The suffering we will begin to look at in this chapter is suffering that has no other cause than our being true to Jesus. And my first question is, "Is such suffering inevitable?"

The answer, whether we like it or not, is: Yes. Jesus himself said it. "Remember the words I spoke to you," he admonished the disciples in his last set of instructions to them. " 'No servant is greater than his master.' If they persecuted me, they will persecute you also. If they obeyed my teaching, they will obey yours also. They will treat you this way because of my name, for they do not know the One who sent me" (Jn 15:20-21). And this reference in John's Gospel is by no means the only one.

So how do we face the suffering? What attitude do we

adopt toward it? Do we ever try to avoid it? In discussing the issue, the best approach is to look at the way Jesus himself handled the suffering he faced, particularly the persecution which he frequently experienced.

When, for instance, did he realize he was destined to suffer? We don't know. We don't even know when he grasped who he was. He seemed as a child to sense a special calling and that he must be in his "Father's house" (Lk 2:49). Yet possibly it was not until he underwent baptism in the River Jordan that a realization broke over him both that he was the *unique* Son from all eternity or that a cruel death awaited him.

The Baptism of Jesus
The baptism of Jesus marked the beginning of his public ministry and perhaps his first premonition of horror ahead. It was therefore a turning point in his life.

His cousin John the Baptist recognized that Jesus did not need to repent of his sins (which is what the baptism by John was all about) and refused to carry it out. But Jesus overcame John's reluctance with the strange words, "Let it be so now; it is proper for us to do this to fulfill all righteousness" (Mt 3:15).

How are we to understand these words? What did he mean by "fulfilling all righteousness?" Three explanations are possible.

The most obvious explanation has to do with baptism itself. Some preachers, in trying to persuade people to get baptized, say he was baptized as a "good example" for us. We are supposed to be baptized because Jesus was.

Yet when a Christian is baptized he is saying something very different from what John's converts were saying when they were baptized. In those days to be baptized was to identify yourself with the person and teaching of the one in whose name you were baptized. By being baptized you were saying, "I want to follow this person's teaching." There is no virtue in the act itself. Thus, the whole point of Christian baptism is that you *align yourself openly with Jesus*. It is an outward confession of your inward commitment to him.

A more obvious explanation is that Jesus, like others in the crowd, felt he had something to repent of. Pure as his life was, his keen conscience was troubled by something that might mean nothing to us but which he, with higher ethical standards, wished publicly to own as sin. In this way he would set for us an example of repentance.

Such a view clashes with what Jesus elsewhere said about himself. It also contradicts what other New Testament writers teach. "Can any of you prove me guilty of sin?" Jesus later demanded of a hostile crowd in the temple (Jn 8:46). The writer to the Hebrews declares to us that Jesus "has been tempted in every way, just as we are—yet was without sin" (Heb 4:15). The New Testament rejects any idea of moral imperfection in Jesus. Consequently, Jesus was not repenting of anything when he got John to baptize him.

The Meaning of Jesus' Baptism
What then was Jesus declaring by being baptized with John's baptism? In the first place he evidently saw it as something God the Father wanted him to do. This would seem the most obvious interpretation of his words, "It is proper for us to do this to fulfill all righteousness." Additionally, his action clearly declares that he approved John's preaching. But, perhaps most important of all, it marks his willingness to *identify himself with sinful humanity*.

He identified with us in the dilemma of our sin, taking his place alongside us as wanting to share the responsibility for our sin. He placed himself where we were. He became our champion by standing in line with us. In Matthew, Luke and John he is seen up to this point as the holy Son of God. From this point on he refers to himself also as the Son of man. The distinction is important—to die as our representative and substitute, he must be both. Only as the Son of man could he represent us. Only as the Son of God could he redeem us.

Yet the step he took is of more than theological interest. It reveals his willingness to suffer shame as well as pain. As we think about it, we are brought up against the wonder of the gospel story. What began with his Incarnation, he here confirms by a second deliberate choice.

And the Incarnation is amazing enough. In it he chose to identify with the major portion of the human race—the poor and the oppressed. Think of God as a diapered baby in a manger. Picture him in the mess of a stinking stable, wind blowing through the cracks in the wall, lying in a manger which is not the last word in cleanliness.

The mind that created the universe is now limited to the body of a human infant. When God is hungry, he cannot even ask in a dignified manner to be fed. He must cry like any other baby and move his little limbs, aimlessly opening and closing tiny fists. His toilet needs must be looked after by others. Angels and demons must have shaken their heads in wonder.

Modern politicians go through empty motions pretending to identify themselves with their constituents. God the Son became in very deed one of us. He could not possibly have been more human. And at the outset of his public ministry he again humbled himself as he stood in line to be baptized with the rest of us.

I am reminded of an experience I had as a medical student. I had missed one of the clinical sessions at a treatment center for venereal diseases. To make up for lost time I was obliged to go to the clinic at night, when medical students did not normally attend. As I entered the door, a strong male nurse took me by the arm and pushed me into a line of shabbily dressed men awaiting treatment.

"Excuse me, I've come to see the doctor in charge," I tried to explain.

"So have all the rest," the nurse replied. "Wait your turn."

"You don't understand. I'm a medical student."

"That's all right, sonny, medical students get it the same way as everyone else."

Eventually, I got him to understand that I was part of the treatment team, not a patient. But I had learned something. I had learned how huge was the chasm between "us" and "them" and how unwilling I was to cross that chasm and identify myself with patients suffering from venereal disease. I have since then been filled with wonder at the chasm Jesus (who knew no sin) crossed to stand beside us sinners, waiting to be baptized.

And it was in response to this action, an action by which he willingly shared our humiliation, that two things occurred. First, the Holy Ghost in the form of a dove (visible at least to John the Baptist and probably to others) descended and rested on Jesus. Second, a voice from heaven was heard to declare, "This is my beloved Son with whom I am well pleased" (Mt 3:17).

The sentence combines two quotations from messianic passages in the Old Testament, one in the Psalms and the other in Isaiah. One announces his sonship, the other his approaching suffering. Psalm 2 has to do with the power and triumph of the Lord's anointed one. From this psalm come the words, "You are my son" (Ps 2:7).

From Isaiah 42:1 come the words "in whom I am well

pleased" or "in whom my soul delights." This chapter contains one of Isaiah's servant passages, the most famous of which is Isaiah 53. Taken as a whole the servant passages give a picture of a faithful servant who will establish righteousness and suffer death, redemptive death, in the process.

While Isaiah 42 does not speak specifically of Messiah's death, there is little doubt in my mind that Jesus was aware of what the quotation implied. He himself chose a servant passage from Isaiah (61) and read it in the synagogue at Nazareth, claiming it referred to him (Lk 4:18-21). And if he was aware that the servant passages referred to him, he would be aware at the time of his baptism that he faced suffering and death (Mt 3:17).

And even if I am mistaken about the words spoken from the skies, it is clear that at a later date Jesus had a vivid grasp of the death he would face. When Peter made his famous confession "You are the Christ, the Son of the living God" (Mt 16:16), we read that "from that time Jesus began to show his disciples that he must go to Jerusalem and suffer many things, and be killed and on the third day be raised" (Mt 16:21).

He was careful to establish in the minds of the disciples the connection between his divinity and his approaching sacrifice. He was the beloved Son, but he was also the suffering servant.

It is important then, as we pursue an understanding of Christian suffering, to inquire what attitude Jesus had to suffering. As we do so, four things stand out: (1) the ferocity with which he rejected any suggestion that he avoid suffering for our redemption, (2) his avoidance of *needless* suffering, (3) his teaching about the paradox of throwing life away only to find it and (4) his insistence that what was true for him applied equally to his followers.

Jesus' Stern Rebuke to Peter

Poor Peter. His confession of Jesus as Christ had been received warmly.

"Blessed are you, Simon Bar-Jona! For flesh and blood has not revealed this to you, but my Father who is in heaven" (Mt 16:17). Peter must have felt both excited and happy. It was only human of him to protest when Jesus stated he must suffer and die. Jesus, always compassionate, might have been expected to correct him gently.

His actual words shake us: "Get behind me, Satan! You are a hindrance to me; for you are not on the side of God, but of men" (Mt 16:23).

Jesus could not have expressed his feelings in stronger terms. Much more is involved than his relationship to Peter, for when Peter, later on, denied Jesus with oaths and cursing, Jesus treated him only with tenderness and love. His shocking response to Peter's protest, then, represents a reaction to the idea Peter expressed. Peter had unwittingly touched on something about which Jesus felt very deeply.

Could Jesus already have felt himself shrinking from the suffering that awaited him? He was human, remember, as well as divine. Did he battle deep in his heart to resist an urge to choose an easier, more comfortable path? This was precisely the suggestion Satan had made to him in the desert. *Jesus would know the origin of Peter's suggestion even if Peter himself did not.* And in the Garden of Gethsemane he cried out to the Father in anguish to show him if there was any other way his mission could be accomplished (Mt 26:36-46). Another time he cried out, "Now is my soul troubled, And what shall I say? 'Father, save me from this hour'? No, for this purpose I have come to this hour" (Jn 12:27).

Suffering was no easier for Jesus (as the last Adam) to face than it is for us. He who "set his face as a flint to go to

Jerusalem" had to overcome every human instinct and resolutely choose a pathway of suffering and death. The ferocity
of his protest was a measure of the internal conflict he faced.
Tempted in all points as we are, he was also tempted to
choose an easier way. But he recognized the temptation as
satanic and one he had first faced in the desert. He sensed the
treachery of the manhood he had assumed, a manhood which
clung to life. He felt the powerful God-given instinct of self-
preservation and overpowered it by an even stronger resolve.
Hence the ferocity of his retort.

Jesus' Avoidance of Needless Suffering

In the eleventh and twelfth chapters of his Gospel, John records the sensation Jesus had created by raising Lazarus from
the dead. The tide of Christ's popularity was running strong.
Everyone clamored to see him. And that very popularity constituted a threat to the authority of the religious leaders. In
an emergency meeting of the Sanhedrin, Caiaphas the High
Priest made it plain that Jesus must die. As Caiaphas saw it,
the death of Jesus would mean that the Jews would avoid
trouble with their Roman rulers. His suggestion quickly
turned into serious planning (Jn 11:45-50). Jesus was aware
of the danger and deliberately sought temporary obscurity in
Ephraim on the edge of the desert.

On another occasion there is a hint that something mirac-
ulous took place when the crowd tried to lay hands on him.
The mob wanted to lynch him and mysteriously Jesus
"walked right through the crowd and went on his way" (Lk
4:30).

If Jesus was resolute in facing death on some occasions, he
was equally quick to avoid it on others. Why? Was he
stronger on some days than others?

The New Testament never suggests that sacrifice and suffering are in themselves good. Jesus faced the cross because it was the only way sinners could be redeemed. He "endured the cross, scorning its shame" (Heb 12:2), not because it was virtuous to do so but because suffering and death were the price he had to pay to achieve his purpose.

This is important. Religious teachers down the ages have taught ascetic techniques, sometimes because making yourself suffer heaps up merit points for you but more often as a kind of Spartan training by which you subdue your rebellious body to a point where you can be truly spiritual. Such suffering is found nowhere in the life of Jesus. Although he was poor, there is no suggestion of asceticism in his lifestyle. Indeed he was accused of being "a glutton and a drunkard" (Mt 11:19) simply because, as he himself acknowledged, he ate and drank like any other person of that day. If he fasted or spent time in prayer, he had a purpose in doing so. He was not training himself to subdue his bodily appetites.

The life of Jesus is totally free of both attitudes to suffering. When finally he faced his passion, it was because "the hour" had come. Jesus was not a masochist, a Spartan, or an ascetic. He faced suffering and death because he loved lost human beings and because there was no other way he could save them.

The Paradox of Life from Death
Although Jesus was aware enough of the danger of his position to avoid running unnecessary risks, he eventually made a public entry into Jerusalem. Passover crowds were seized with a wild surge of enthusiasm.

Cloaks and palm leaves were strewn on the roadway as he approached the city riding a young ass (Jn 12:12-19). Some of the sensation doubtless went back to the incident in Bethany when Jesus raised Lazarus from the dead (Jn 11:38-44). In the temple, even foreign visitors were inquiring after him (Jn 12:20-22). A lesser person might have become intoxicated enough with popular acclaim to try to ride to power on the crest of the wave. But when Philip brought Jesus the message that Greek visitors were inquiring after him, he responded with an ecstasy of a different kind.

"The hour has come for the Son of Man to be glorified" (Jn 12:23), he said. Did he mean that he had it made? Did he feel there was enough popular support for him to swing an armed revolution? The words that follow dispel any such idea: "I tell you the truth, unless a kernel of wheat falls to the ground and dies, it remains only a single seed. But if it dies, it produces many seeds" (Jn 12:24). To be glorified, then, is not to ride popularity to a position of power but to give one's life fruitfully.

Jesus is going to win power not by grasping for it, but by laying down his life for others. Indeed, throwing away one's life is the only way to find it. "The man who loves his life will lose it, while the man who hates his life in this world will keep it for eternal life" (Jn 12:25).

By weakness and defeat
He won the mead and crown—
Trod all His foes beneath His feet
By being trodden down.[9]

We have already seen however that Jesus is not teaching that suffering is in itself virtuous. He was guided by a dual principle—obedience to the Father and love for humankind. Both principles demanded that when the time was ripe he must face the cross. However painful it might prove and however much he would shrink from it in horror, he was determined to face all it involved—to be the kernel of wheat and fall into the ground and die. He was ready to hate his own life.

To "hate" in this context means to value something else

infinitely more than life. Faced with a choice between preserving your life and obeying God, you choose obedience. You choose it because your relationship to God is more important than life. Jesus did not hate his life out of bitterness or depression. He hated it in the sense that he *scorned the idea of clinging to life* when so much else was at stake.

But there could be different reasons for his willingness to face death. Schweitzer and others have suggested that Jesus welcomed the thought of the cross for psychological reasons. Believing himself to be Messiah and yet perceiving that he must inevitably be defeated in a conflict with Jewish and Roman authorities, Jesus resolved the tension between external reality and inner conviction by seeing himself as the sacrificial Lamb of God. In this way he did not have to give up his belief in his divinity but could go happily to his death believing himself to be the Savior of the world.

There is an a priori assumption in this view. It is that Jesus was only human; that he was not in fact God Incarnate. It is assumed that he was struggling and growing in an attempt to understand God as well as to understand his own person and the human dilemma. The solution at which he eventually arrives is forged in the stress of bewildering circumstances. It is also a psychotic solution. No one would say this, but it makes Jesus out to be a crazy man.

If, however, Jesus is indeed God, the whole picture changes. No complex theory of Christ's internal resolution of stressful problems is necessary. Why then do I mention the view? I mention it because some of us may in fact give way to suffering because at times it is easier to do so than to face misunderstanding or interpersonal difficulties.

Suffering can at times be an escapist solution. Theologians have probably read into the actions of Jesus psychological weaknesses of their own.

For instance, one morning in our hotel, the waiter had served my wife's breakfast but not mine. I had been given orange juice and coffee but nothing else. "Signal to him." my wife said. "Don't just sit there." However, I had seen how busy the waiter was and had observed other guests treating him rudely. I was reluctant to create a fuss.

Yet, if I am honest, I have to confess that my reluctance did not arise from consideration for the waiter but from simple cowardice. I didn't want the waiter to dislike me. I was willing to give up my breakfast rather than offend him.

Now I suppose I could have fooled myself into believing I was being spiritual. I was sacrificing my rights. I was being a "doormat for the Lord." But to have done so would be to have done precisely what some theologians maintain Jesus did when facing the cross—take the psychologically easiest course. As a matter of fact, I got up from the table, went over to the waiter, and politely told him about his mistake.

Jesus never dodged tough issues, and he never taught his followers to do so. He faced embarrassing issues squarely, and on one significant occasion, violently. Jesus will not countenance "suffering" under the guise of spirituality when such suffering is in fact an escape from an embarrassing situation.

Jesus was altogether healthy in his attitude to sacrifice and suffering. He hated them. He shrank from them. Yet he chose them deliberately because there was no other way to redeem us.

His motivation in choosing death was that he anticipated joy and triumph beyond it: "who for the joy set before him endured the cross" (Heb 12:2). In his brief talk with Philip in John 12, Jesus is very clear about the fact that the kernel of wheat that fell into the ground and died *brought forth much fruit.* There was no other point in being a kernel of wheat. He also made it very clear that a general principle is involved—namely, that by holding our lives lightly, by seeking the will of God above life itself, we learn the qualitative difference between existence and true and eternal living. By facing death we start to live.

It is sentimental to view the crucified Jesus as a lovely model of passive anguish. In truth he is an active conqueror, grappling powerfully with sin and death. He is our champion, scorning his own life that he might batter down the prison doors and set captives free.

He Hell, in Hell laid low.
Made sin, He sin o'erthrew,
Bowed to the grave, destroyed it so
And death, by dying, slew.
Bless, bless the Conqueror slain!
Slain in His victory!
Who lived, Who died, Who lives again
For thee, His Church for thee![10]

There is nothing morbid about the sacrifice of Jesus. The music of the Passion must be written in a major, not a minor, key. He looked on the travail of his soul and was well pleased. He saw beyond his death to the army of the redeemed, drawn to him in salvation when he was lifted up. And though he sweated great drops of blood, though he knew spiritual and physical agony, his death was the death of a strong man binding the god of this world. We speak of him as the Lamb of God to remind ourselves of his purity, not of his passivity. We do well to remember that he is also the Lion of the tribe of Judah.

Following Jesus

The principles which were true of Jesus must also be true of us if we wish to follow him: "If anyone would come after me, he must deny himself and take up his cross daily and follow me" (Lk 9:23). I shall devote the rest of the book to dealing with this monumental principle. But as we come to the end of the chapter, let me enunciate the basic principle of interpretation and summarize what I have said so far.

In the previous chapter I defined Christian suffering as excluding three types of suffering—the common suffering all persons are exposed to because we live in a fallen world; the sufferings that arise from our own sin and stupidity; and disciplinary sufferings, those painful experiences by which we grow in faith and in grace. I limited Christian suffering to that suffering which arises as one of the direct consequences of following Jesus Christ closely.

The distinctions I have made may be a little artificial. For instance, painful experiences that arise from my own stupidity can contribute to my spiritual growth. I can learn from my mistakes. Again, pain that comes to me as a result of my being close to Christ can have the same beneficial results in my life. Nevertheless, the distinction is important since before deciding to follow Christ closely I must count the cost. I must recognize that in some sense I face death all the time.

I must also recognize that the attitudes that Jesus had to suffering will serve as a model for me as I face suffering too. He faced redemptive suffering with fierce resolve, seeing as Satanic anything that would turn him aside. But he saw no virtue in suffering for suffering's sake, and he avoided it where possible. Moreover, his outlook on suffering was not morbid, neurotic or masochistic. He saw beyond the pain to glory and victory. And it was the prospect of glory to the Father, of salvation for humanity and of victory over darkness that impelled him to overcome the shrinking of his flesh and to march forward resolutely, trampling death under his feet.

We are invited to walk in the steps of a conqueror.

Questions for Individuals or Groups

1. From your own experience do you agree with the author's statement that for Christians suffering for Jesus is inevitable?

2. How is the meaning of Jesus' baptism explained on pages 79-81? Do you agree or disagree with this approach? Explain.

3. At what point in your life did you make an outward confession of your commitment to Christ—by baptism, joining a church, witnessing to a friend or in some other way?

4. Why did Jesus react so strongly to Peter in Matthew 16:23 (pp. 82-84)? Have you ever been tempted by your well-meaning Christian friends to avoid a task God has called you to? Explain.

5. Why do you think that Jesus chose to avoid the crowd in Luke 4:30? In what kinds of situations should we avoid needless suffering (pp. 84-85)?

6. What does it mean for you personally to throw away your life in order to find it?

7. How can you identify with the author's story about not being served breakfast, but suffering rather than calling the waiter (p. 88)? Have you ever used your Christianity as an excuse for avoiding a difficult situation? Explain.

8. Why is it important that we view Christ on the cross as an active conqueror, rather than as a passive sacrifice (p. 89)?

9. When have you been able to see beyond suffering to the ultimate victory?

10. How have chapters five and six helped you to understand suffering in your life?

7

Take
Up Your
Cross

I cannot stress strongly enough that there is no virtue in suffering itself. It makes no sense to choose to suffer when you don't have to. You prove nothing by lying across a railroad track and letting the train amputate one of your legs. But if, in rescuing a child from peril, you lose a leg, then the amputation, disastrous as it may be, constitutes a badge of sacrificial courage and a reminder of the value of a human life. Such suffering has merit.

When Jesus tells you to take up your cross daily, he is not telling you to find some way to suffer daily. He is simply forewarning of what happens to the person committed to following him. The phrase has no mystical significance. It is neither a call to seek suffering as an end in itself nor an invitation to undergo an inner experience of dying. "If you want to follow me," he is saying, "be prepared for what you will have to face. They put me on a cross—and they may do the same to you. They ridiculed me—they will ridicule you. You will do well, then, to arm yourself daily with a willingness to take whatever may come to you because of me."

If we face the cost of following Jesus realistically, and if we face it every day, we will in fact face a deeper kind of dying, a "kernel of wheat" kind of dying. We will die to the lives we once wanted to live. We will die to our right to control what happens to us, to our ambitions, our right to choose, indeed to every "right" we think we have. We must therefore look at both aspects of commitment to Jesus—the risk of unpleasant things happening, and the deeper question of the death that must precede the experience of resurrection life here and now.

Let me begin with the risk of unpleasantness. In the Gospels Jesus points this out a number of times. "I am sending you out like sheep among wolves," he told the disciples. "Therefore be as shrewd as snakes and as innocent as doves. . . . All men will hate you because of me. . . . A student is not above his teacher, nor a servant above his master. . . . If the head of the house has been called Beelzebub, how much more the members of his household" (Mt 10:16-25). In other words, whenever you do something Jesus may send you to do, you will get the treatment Jesus got—sometimes acceptance, sometimes rejection. You will be treated as he was treated. Some people will be drawn to you as bees to honey. Others will hate the ground you stand on.

Again, in his last discourse to the apostles: "Remember the words I spoke to you: 'No servant is greater than his master.' If they persecuted me, they will persecute you also. They will treat you this way because of my name" (Jn 15:20-21).

If you are open and honest—true to yourself and true to Christ—your life will provoke hostility in some and will powerfully attract others. To some it will be "a savour of life unto life" and to others "of death unto death". If you are faithful to him, it may make you unpopular and unprosperous. Of course, it may have the opposite effect too. The question is: Do you, in fact, put Christ first, whatever the relative cost?

Avoidable Suffering

We must not, however, be "gluttons for punishment." Jesus does not urge his followers passively to accept any persecution that comes their way. "When you are persecuted in one place, flee to another," he tells them (Mt 10:23). In the context in which it is found, "Take up your cross" means something similar to "Take your life in your hands." It means: "Be prepared to carry your own noose around with you, to run the risk of anything, even death itself. Don't seek death. Avoid it if you can, and get the gospel message to anyone who will listen. If men threaten you, go someplace else where they will listen."

During the fifteenth and sixteenth centuries, the Roman Catholic Church rightly opposed a doctrine of some mystics that became known as quietism. Quietists taught that since God is sovereign, everything that comes to us comes directly from God. And quietists went on to say that we should therefore resist nothing we encounter in life, but receive whatever comes quietly and without any resistance. We must receive everything from God as part of his training for us. To resist suffering is to resist God.

At first it might seem that this was precisely what I was saying in the previous chapter when I discussed the disciplinary suffering God sends into our lives. Not so. I may certainly trust God about everything I encounter. Certainly he accepts the responsibility for the fact that it has touched my life. Certainly I must thank him for the fact that even in that circumstance he will be faithful to me and bring good out of it. But he does not expect me to be passive in the face of evil. When he tells me not to resist evil but to return good for evil, he is not telling me to let thugs beat an old lady to death, or to take no steps to deal with my headache.

When I worked in the casualty ward of a busy hospital, both women and men would be brought to us after having been beaten up by their spouses. Some were seriously injured. We would tell them that it was our custom to alert the police. But since the police were only able to help when the victim would testify, we would ask whether they were willing to inform the police about what had happened. Very few would.

I recall many a woman, her eyes haunted by dread, who would repeatedly refuse help. If the social worker offered to find her shelter she might accept, but after having gone to the shelter would return for the innumerable time to her husband to be beaten again.

Even when, as a psychiatrist, I offered such a couple the opportunity for counselling and help, the victim would often refuse to collaborate. Occasionally, a Christian woman would say, her voice filled with depression, "It is probably my fault. I must do a better job of obeying him." And male victims were too ashamed of being seen as weak to want to do anything about it.

Not to take some action, especially after repeated provocation, is to foster evil and to invite more. In some cases the violence of a drunken husband was directed against the children also, so that their lives were in ongoing jeopardy as well as that of the mother. It is true that Jesus tells us to return evil with good, but sometimes the good must take the form of removing the temptation to do evil out of a violent person's way.

Sharing Christ's Suffering

But in addition to avoidable and unnecessary suffering, there is true suffering for Christ. Living as we do in an age of tolerance and political freedom, we forget the risks many Christians have run in other times and places. Today in Eastern Europe, Cuba, Russia, China and parts of the Muslim world, faithfulness to Christ costs. To us the plight of our brothers and sisters may seem remote. We should remember that the degree of tolerance and freedom we know in the West is unparalleled in world history. As little as fifty years ago there was less religious toleration than exists in the West today. Yet already grave signs are apparent. We have now passed the point of greatest freedom. The sun of freedom has passed its zenith, and who knows when it may set.

Historically, the crucifixion of Jesus set in motion a chain reaction of harassments, imprisonments and martyrdoms for his followers that has continued to this day. In most parts of the world for most of the past two thousand years, followers of Christ have risked imprisonment and death. The light of freedom has waxed and waned many times. Sometimes Christians have gone to their deaths by thousands and have done so singing the praises of the Lamb upon the throne. At other times they have enjoyed more liberty.

It would be foolish of us to assume that our present luxurious freedom will continue indefinitely. Our current freedom is the delayed end result of the Reformation with its biblical view of humanity. As the biblical influence wanes, it is likely that freedom will not continue. There are signs that the conditions necessary for tolerance and freedom are already being eroded. Democracy is a fragile flower of late bloom (it was, in its present form, completely unknown to the Greeks), likely to be withered by the scorching winds of impatient hate.

It is therefore important that we all ask ourselves, "Am I willing to risk imprisonment and death for Christ?" Many professing believers are not willing. As tyrannical and anti-religious regimes (both left-wing and right-wing) have sprung up around the world in the twentieth century, prominent Christian leaders and established Christian institutions living under them have shown too great a readiness to "cooperate" with Caesar. Others have fled prematurely out of fear of what *might* happen under another regime. On the other hand, an uncooperative minority has found itself stripped of the civil liberties we take so much for granted.

Where would we stand if we had to face what Christians faced in Nazi Germany in World War 2 or more recently in China and Cuba? The invitation is subtle. No one is asked to renounce Christ—only to put him in his proper place, second to people and state. The pressure is fierce. "Perhaps if I cooperate from within, I will be able to influence them more" is the argument of many. The church in the first century was exposed to similar temptations. In such a world Christ calls us, as he called them, to pick up our nooses daily and follow him.

I do not wish to be an alarmist about what it costs to be faithful to Christ. Yet I feel I must point both to Scripture and to the course of church history. I want to awaken the Western church with the blast of a trumpet, warning her that the normal conditions under which the church bears witness are not those we now experience, but are conditions adverse to Christian witness. I believe that the darkness may be descending again, and I fear that few of us are prepared for it. We belong to a long tradition of martyrdom, but we have become soft and ill-prepared.

"Dear friends, do not be surprised," writes Peter, "at the painful trial you are suffering, as though something strange were happening to you. But rejoice that you participate in the sufferings of Christ, so that you may be overjoyed when his glory is revealed. . . . However, if you suffer as a Christian, do not be ashamed, but praise God that you bear that name" (1 Pet 4:12-13, 16).

Peter gives three reasons why we should be happy to suffer for Christ. In the first place we should rejoice because we are sharing his sufferings with him. We should also be glad because we will share in his glory. Finally, suffering is a sign that God's Spirit is manifest in our lives.

But let us be clear about one thing. We cannot call our suffering for Christ's sake "redemptive." We are not taking on their behalf the suffering other people deserve. Yet there is a sense in which we are suffering for the sake of others. We are suffering so that they might see and know Christ. In this way we share the sufferings of the One who hungered, experienced weariness, was mocked, maligned and spat upon, all because he sought to help his persecutors.

Whenever his followers experience hostility or hardships for the same reason, they are truly sharing Christ's suffering. We walk with him, and the abuse that falls on him falls also on us.

And this sharing creates new bonds. Read *Foxe's Book of Martyrs* (if you can stomach it) or Merle D'Aubigne's *History of the Reformation*, and you will be astonished at the buoyant rejoicing of persecuted Christians in former ages. Their joy amazes us. Tortures that would have reduced us to jabbering idiots left them still praising God. We cannot see ourselves showing anything like the same temerity and fortitude.

What we fail to realize is that to share Christ's sufferings is also to draw near to him. And to draw near to him, be the outward circumstances what they may, is to be filled with joy. Like Stephen as rocks battered his fragile frame, we see heaven opened and know that things are not what they appear to be. In such circumstances it becomes easier to pray for our enemies.

Christians will never go through the black night Christ passed through. That was for him alone. But we shall enjoy his nearness in those parts of his suffering in which we are privileged to share. We need have no fear of them.

Sharing Christ's Glory

I pointed out earlier that when Christ suffered, his eyes were fixed on "the joy that was set before him." He looked forward to "bearing much fruit." In the same way Christians must look beyond suffering to the glory that awaits them. "If we endure, we will also reign with him" (2 Tim 2:12).

Some halo hunters feel it ignoble to be concerned about rewards when they suffer for Christ. They tell us it would be more spiritual to suffer without any thought of reward. After all Christ has done for us, no suffering is too great to undergo for him. True. Yet if he offers reward, who among us will turn up their nose at the magnanimity of the King of Glory? And since the Scripture records such promises for our encouragement and hope, why not keep the promises before our eyes lest the day of testing throw us?

Rewards in Scripture are promised for all forms of faithfulness, but especially for faithfulness in suffering. We do not fully understand what form the rewards will take. Crowns may symbolize increased responsibility. To some the words will be uttered, "Enter into the joy of Lord." Whatever the rewards may be, we are fools to do anything but cherish the thought of winning them.

Commitment to Christ in Hong Kong

So how do we begin to face the question in our own lives?

How would you react, for instance, if you were a Chinese citizen of Hong Kong? In 1997 the control of the city reverts to the government of mainland China. As I write, 1997 still lies in the future, and while many people and organizations are frantically making as much money as they can while capitalism still exists, others, and these include Christian organizations and churches, grow increasingly fearful. Will the same fate await them as awaited the church in China?

The greater proportion of older and well-established pastors have already left the city, responding to invitations from Chinese congregations in other parts of the world. This has created a significant gap in the leadership of the Hong Kong Christian community so that an unaccustomed degree of responsibility has fallen on much younger shoulders. In the fall of 1988 I addressed the annual conference of pastors of the Alliance church in Hong Kong and was astonished by the youthfulness of the present crop of pastors.

Many Christians cannot leave Hong Kong. Lacking money, desirable qualifications or an invitation to leave the city, they are stuck with whatever conditions prevail. When I ask Christians whether they plan to leave or to stay, I get three kinds of answers. Some look resigned and say, "I cannot leave." Others tell me of their plans to leave. Yet others say: "No, we feel it is our duty to stay, even though conditions may be very difficult. This is our community, the community among whom we are called to witness. We are called to pray for the good of our city" (see Jer 33:4-7). For these Christians, a city under alien and perhaps hostile control, is a city whose wellbeing (in the deepest sense) they must continue to seek.

Dr. Philemon Choi has given up the financial rewards of medical practice to head a Christian organization called Breakthrough, a powerful and influential voice for Christianity in the city. He lives on a small salary in a cramped apartment with his wife and two sons. Members of Breakthrough feel that, since they do not know what conditions will prevail, they must take the risk of staying in Hong Kong after 1997, doing whatever they can both to help Christians in their faith and to spread the Good News of the Kingdom.

Jackie Pullinger, on the other hand, is not Chinese but British. She could leave any time, but has no plans to leave—ever. She heads up St. Stephen's Society, a significant work based in the so-called Walled City. For years she has ministered in a Mother Teresa-like fashion to drug-addicted members of the triads (or Chinese secret societies and gangs), to prostitutes in wretched conditions there, as well as to the city's homeless.

Living inside the Walled City in a single room, in an area shut off from the light of the sun, she has again and again seen God deliver triad members from their sin and from many years of heroin addiction and crime. Several camps and homes in the colony now minister to recovering addicts. She moves in the power of Christ.

So Jackie will stay. She feels she must not abandon those who are poor, enslaved and wretched. Both Philemon Choi and Jackie Pullinger are seeking to follow Christ fully, and have faced realistically the cost of so doing. Both have won the recognition and respect of the Hong Kong government, and in addition Jackie has won the respect of the police and even of the triad leaders. But what may be honor now has come at the cost of suffering and misunderstanding in the past, and could in any case become the very opposite of honor under another regime.

Take Up Your Cross

Perhaps it is time I answered the question I asked a moment ago—how can you begin?

I can think of two ways. The first thing to do is to face the issues as realistically as possible in your mind. Begin with a special time of prayer, sitting rather than kneeling—you can spend longer thinking and will be less likely to tire physically that way. Ask God to help you see the issues clearly as they affect you.

The second step is to try to put yourself in the shoes of some of the people we have been talking about. Face with them (after all, you are part of the same body of Christ as they are) the risks and uncertainties they face. Ask yourself, "Would I be faithful, or would I find some excuse not to do as they are doing?" Don't be surprised if you feel fear and self-doubt. That will only indicate that you are facing the issues realistically. Most people who do so experience self-doubt.

Do not let the self-doubt get to you, however. You see, you do not live in Hong Kong and are not yet called to face what others are actually facing. You are being tested and trained now in smaller ways. If you are faithful in little things while freedom lasts, chances are that you will be faithful when the big tests come. There is valuable training in faithfulness where you are now.

Recently in Waikiki I watched surfers from beginners to experts. Some balanced gracefully on long and expensive boards bigger than themselves, riding for unbelievable distances with an enviable ease and style. Others were youngsters nearer the shore with short, stubby boards, learning to body surf and to pick up the skill of selecting the right wave and the right moment to get in sync with it.

Two things were clear to me. One was that the ideal way to learn surfing is as a youngster, on small waves near the shore, with a beaten-up scrap of surfboard. The big waves come later. The second thing that became clear was that there's an exhilaration in the learning. Otherwise, why would kids and adults alike go back again and again for more? Surfers are not masochists.

It is the same in following Christ. You learn best with the little waves right in front of you. Ask God to show you which they are. Commit yourself to learning on them. If you do so, you will begin to experience the exhilaration that comes with the mastery of a new skill and with it a longing to go for bigger stuff. You will have begun to experience the joy of following him fully.

Questions for Individuals and Groups

1. What "rights" are hard for you to give up to Christ (p. 94)? How do you put your personal desires aside?

2. How do you react to the Quietists' theology of suffering (pp. 95-96)? When have you seen evidence of this attitude in the church?

3. On page 96 the author says, "Not to take some action, especially after repeated provocation, is to foster evil and to invite more." How can you integrate an active response to evil into your faith?

4. Do you agree with the author that the church in the West will be oppressed again? Explain. If there was to be persecution, how do think you'd react?

5. The author suggests reading *Foxe's Book of Martyrs* or *History of the Reformation* to understand what it's like to suffer as a Christian. How do you react to these stories or others you have heard about Christian martyrs?

6. What does the idea of sharing Christ's glory mean to you?

7. How did you feel when you read the stories of Philemon Choi and Jackie Pullinger (pp. 101-102)?

8. Even though you probably don't face the trials of Christians in Hong Kong, how do you think you are being tested right now?

9. How are you willing to begin working to build the kingdom today, even if it requires suffering?

8

Christians,
the Law
and Persecution

*C*hrist's presence on earth provoked devotion in some people and resentment in others. The masses were swayed between two extremes—sometimes blindly enthusiastic and at other times blindly hostile. True Christianity always provokes the same reactions. It has been said of the apostle Paul that wherever he went there was either a riot or a revival.

Whenever the Spirit of God is present in power, people react. At times the reaction will be hostile. But if it is, we are commanded to rejoice because, as Peter tells us, "the Spirit of glory and of God rests" upon us (1 Pet 4:14). Nowadays, the only reaction we anticipate as a result of the Spirit's presence is mass conversions. It never occurs to us that persecution may also indicate God's power.

Peter is very specific, however. The suffering he refers to is suffering "because of the name of Christ" (1 Pet 4:13).

Christians sometimes suffer because of their arrogance or stupidity. You must have observed it yourself sometimes. Some pig-headed enthusiasts "witness," not with courtesy and out of love, but from a need to triumph. They win arguments but lose people. The history of true revivals is replete with stories of the damaging effects of men and women whose carnal excesses (which they mistook for devotion to Christ) hindered the work of God. Such people are also persecuted. They ask for it.

Similarly, governments can be arrogant and stupid in relation to other governments—all in the name of Christ. And when they are, both the government and its people suffer. Mistaken enthusiasm on the part of governments leads to "Christian" wars. Take the Crusades, for example. Not all so-called Christian endeavors have been so clearly unchristian, yet all of these wars seemed—to the people who fought them—to be indisputably for Christ. Soldiers suffered and died "for Christ." Their suffering resulted from wrong thinking. They and their leaders misunderstood the nature of faith.

But suffering can truly be suffering for and with Christ. And this is always so when the issue is the proclamation of the gospel. A year or so ago I arrived with a team in Penang, Malaysia, where we were to conduct seminars both in Penang itself and in Kuala Lumpur. Malaysia's government is Muslim, and the object of the seminars was to equip churches for evangelism.

When we were driven from the airport to meet the Malaysian Christian leaders at one of their homes, we were immediately faced with a serious question, "Are you willing to take the risk of continuing with the seminars?"

We had arrived at a time of national emergency. Public meetings were banned and the status of meetings such as our seminars was unclear. People perceived as enemies of the regime were being arrested, and among them were some Christian leaders. At that point no one was certain where the prisoners were being held or what their fate would be. Church members were afraid.

What was the real question in the minds of those leaders who asked the question? Were they asking whether we were willing to suffer, or did they themselves have fears? Were they perhaps looking for a way of telling us that it would have been better for them if we had not come? After all, it was their country, and the risks they faced were far greater than the risks we faced ourselves. We said, "You are the ones who must make that decision. The worst that could happen to us would be a day or two of prison followed by expulsion from the country. That much we will cheerfully face. Your own fates could be much worse."

The leaders glanced at one another and smiled. They had already decided what Christ wanted them to do. "We want to go ahead," they said.

Fortunately, we experienced no difficulty. True, there was one day when police watched from their vehicles as we entered and left the building. But there were no incidents, and God greatly blessed the meetings.

The Gospel and the State

There are times then when persecution may come from the State. The church began when imperial Rome ruled the Mediterranean basin. The day came when Christians were faced with the question of whether they were to acknowledge Caesar or Jesus as God. Some Christians refused openly to worship Caesar and suffered imprisonment, torture and death. Others kept their Christian faith secret.

And ever since, almost continuously and often in many

places at once, Christians have been faced with the choice of remaining faithful to Christ and being persecuted by the State, or of denying their faith when challenged and avoiding suffering. In recent years, across the world, countless numbers of Christians have suffered death and imprisonment in China, Russia, Chile, Albania, several African countries, Muslim countries and many others. For example, Pastor Lam of China, whom I introduced in chapter one, was imprisoned for Christ and did hard labor in the mines for twenty-five years.

Your pulse may beat more quickly when you imagine what you would do if times become difficult. But in the West as I write, times are not difficult. We enjoy freedom unparalleled in history. But, as noted, this could be changing.

In the United States, for instance, ever since the tragedy of Jonestown small legislative changes have shifted the government's position from one of being the watchdog and guardian of religious freedom, to one of protecting society as a whole from religious groups and cults which are harmful to the public. And though the shift has had little perceptible impact on the religious freedom of evangelical Christians, it is a relatively short step to increased religious intolerance.

Christian writers with an inadequate grasp of church history, sometimes define the term *cult* in a way that would fit the more radical Christian groups of the past, or almost any revival in its formative stages. The day may come when groups God himself has raised up will get stuck with the label *dangerous cult*. It is important, therefore, that we look carefully at the Bible's teaching on our relationship with the State.

Some countries go so far as to forbid Christian belief itself. More commonly Christians are forbidden to "proselytize." Yet, to be a Christian at all is to confess and to proclaim Christ. The New Testament knows no silent Christianity.

Under such conditions, what are Christians to do?

More commonly in the West, Christians have been imprisoned for their adherence to specific (but often disputed) points of their faith—for example, pacifism, unwillingness to join trade unions, and protests over civil liberties and nuclear arms. As I write, Christians are being jailed for obstructing access to abortion clinics.

It is not at present clear which way the battle of prolife versus prochoice will go. What is clear is that state governments in the U.S. and provincial governments in Canada are prepared to imprison any Christians who defy the law by doing what they believe (rightly or wrongly) to be obedience to Christ.

In this book it would be inappropriate for me to discuss the controversies arising over the details of what being a Christian involves. Rather, I must urge on all of us the cost that is always involved, however we may conceive of our Christian duty. Here I must confine myself to general principles.

Faith and the Power of the Lie

Some Christians feel we must always obey the State, others that we should be quick to disobey, even in a democracy, when we perceive that the State is in error. What does Scripture teach?

Paul tells us, "The authorities that exist have been established by God. Consequently, he who rebels against the authority is rebelling against what God has instituted, and those who do so will bring judgement on themselves" (Rom 13:1-2). Paul wrote in a time of corrupt and often cruel authorities who implemented crucifixion and who approved of slavery. Yet because they were God-appointed, they were to be obeyed.

Yet, there is a tension in Scripture. John plainly sees the

evil hand of Satan behind the State. When he and Peter stood before the State-backed Sanhedrin, they posed the question, "Are we to obey God or you guys?" (my wording!). Their answer made it plain that a Christian must sometimes defy the State.

The Pauline principle represents the general rule. Authority, even morally imperfect authority, is good. If Satan really had his way, there would be anarchy and chaos. In his mercy God backs authority, for the worst and most tyrannical of governments is more desirable than chaos. So in general we obey civil authority.

But John is telling us what will happen to Christians who always obey God, and why. As we have seen, there will be times when obeying the State will mean disobeying God. There is no disagreement between John and Paul. John merely looks at the other side of the question. Behind the power of the State he also sees the ruler of this world, Satan. As the ruler of this world, Satan will manipulate human government to defy God and to persecute his people, especially when God's people advance the cause of the kingdom of God.

The image he uses is that of the Beast, which seems in Revelation to represent human political power. The Beast rises "out of the sea" (Rev 13:1). To John the sea seems to symbolize the mass of humanity. Thus human political power is seen to rise up from out of the masses. The Beast has seven crowned heads and ten horns—an indication of its Satanic nature. And the dragon (clearly identified by John in Revelation 12:1-12 as Satan) gives to the Beast "his power and his throne and great authority" (Rev 13:2).

These are two aspects of government and the State that in Scripture are held in tension. Both are true. We must take both Paul and John seriously. God has permitted human political power to exist even though it is demonic. Insofar as the

State opposes the advance of the Kingdom, civil disobedience is sometimes called for. But when and under what circumstances? How do we understand the two principles in practice? When do we bow to Caesar, and when do we defy the Beast?

Involved in the tension is the mystery of God's sovereignty. Both God's and Satan's power are involved in every event the newspapers record. History reflects inconceivable battles "in heavenly places." It puzzles us that there should be any battle at all. God's power and his authority are limitless. They spring from his holy being. Satan is merely one of his creations and Satan's power, though great, is limited. Why doesn't God simply wipe the Satanic hosts out? Unlike Satan, he is omniscient and omnipresent. What is stopping him?

An important aspect of God's holiness is his truth. He is the God of truth, the source of all truth. Satan gained his authority over us because we believed a lie, *for there is no power in a lie until it is believed.* So Satan has limited power. But at the dawn of human history, we believed a lie and the terrible consequence of that belief was that we fell under its power. God, respecting our dignity as those created in his image, allows us to suffer the consequences of wrong belief in a Satanic lie. He let us lie in the bed we have made, follow the path we have chosen. We are to learn from our experience—and what a lesson it has been! And that which has no power in itself (the lie) is now seen to have awesome power when it is accepted.

In ordaining that we should suffer the consequences, God did not cease to be sovereign over the earth. Nor did he abandon the world to the unchecked malice of Satan. He loves us. His sovereignty imposes strict limits on Satan's power on this earth. And since Satan's power resides in lies and deception, God has opposed it in human history by systematically revealing more and more truth to us. One aim God has is to overcome Satan *through us*, believing and proclaiming truth. For he is "the father of lies" (Jn 8:44) and the serpent that "will go out to deceive the nations" (Rev 20:8) with his principal power springing from those abilities. Wherever lies and deception are accepted, Satan's rule grows stronger. Wherever truth is revealed, believed and acted on, the Kingdom prevails. Truth becomes vivid in Jesus and his teaching. If we hold to it, we will know the truth, and the truth will make us free (Jn 8:32).

When I was a medical student, I bathed in the men's residence. The building was an old one, and in the basement there was an extra large, old-fashioned bathtub which was a favorite of ours. I usually enjoy luxuriating in a tub of steaming water, but one particular day I was puzzled and troubled.

I wondered why God had never answered my prayers to deliver me from a particular sin into which I fell repeatedly. I would fall, repent, be reconciled and repeat it with monotonous regularity and bitter discouragement. I had attended special meetings, had tried, then trusted, and told myself, "Not I, but Christ." I had adopted every technique that Christianity at the time could offer me. I had even travelled to Switzerland to ask a particular Bible teacher how one "died with Christ." Truth (if truth it was) was not making me free.

"Why bother any more?" I thought, and relaxed in the bath to let my troubles ease away. Suddenly the words came, "You have died with Christ." That was all. I stopped lounging and sat up. "Did the Bible actually say that?"

I forgot about the water. I had not even begun to wash myself. Possessed by a new urgency, I got out of the tub, pulled a large bath towel round me, and hurried to my room. I lit the old-fashioned gas fire quickly and pulled my Bible from the bookshelf.

I had died with Christ? I was dead? I found what I was looking for in Romans: "We died to sin; how can we live in it any longer? . . . Now if we died with Christ, we believe that we will also live with him" (Rom 6:2, 8). I read the passage again and again. Suddenly it seemed to me that I had been pacing the walls of *a cell that didn't exist.* Or if it did exist, it only existed because I believed a lie. It existed in my mind, not in reality. The truth washed through me with a brilliant rush of light, and I found that the walls of my cell were gone and I was walking (indeed, had been walking all along) on the open hillside. I had not known I was free. The cell was not reality. The hillside was. Now the whole hillside was mine.

And so it proved instantly. I was then and thereafter, free.

But there is a catch. The Holy Spirit had brought the words to me. They had come to me anointed by his power. Because he brought them to me, they came not merely to my head but penetrated the depths of my heart.

We are in ourselves more vulnerable to lies than we are to truth. We may have a head grasp of a principle while its power eludes us. Truth is more powerful than lies. Its power remains even if it is not believed. But propositional truth alone, even biblical propositional truth, is not enough. Truth is a Person. He comes among us in this age as the Holy Spirit who is the Spirit of Truth.

Therefore the principal weapon of our warfare against the Beast will always be the proclamation of biblical truth under the presence and power of the Holy Spirit.

We must never avoid social issues. But when the church is more concerned about implementing the social implications of the gospel than about proclamation of the gospel in its power, then the church will fail to advance the kingdom and change society. Under those circumstances social problems will not diminish, but will multiply. History itself demonstrates this.

Satan's power is really extraordinarily limited. He can only gain control over us to the extent that we believe lies—and the same holds true of communities and therefore of governments and the State. We hand power to Satan, power he has no ability to take by force, whenever we believe a lie.

But that lie has been believed. Western governments are more and more influenced by nonbiblical values.

The Changing Situation

There has been a shift in government policies as certain ideas—commonly labelled *liberal* these days, but ideas to which no particular label can be attached—permeate society.

We no longer live in a Christian society. In fact we never have. We must therefore think through the issues clearly. We must know what constitutes obedience to Christ and what constitutes playing the martyr before an imaginary angelic host. There is such a thing as cowardly disloyalty to Christ. How can we know the difference?

Even those of us who are not facing civil disobedience right now must face the question: What does it mean to take up your cross and follow Jesus? What does it mean to have two loyalties, a primary loyalty to God and a secondary loyalty to Caesar?

But the question is wrongly expressed. To be committed to Jesus is to have one loyalty only. Loyalty is always a virtue, and my loyalty to the State is an integral part of my loyalty to him. I am to be faithful to my country in precisely the same way that he is faithful to it. In general, as his follower, I must obey its laws. But there will be times when I oppose them, and other times when, out of loyalty, I will even disobey them. But again, when?

At least we can see now what is important. If the reason we have been left here is to serve Christ and advance his kingdom, and if our task is best conceived as one of overcoming Satanic lies with truth, then clearly the proclamation of biblical truth in Jesus is our priority. The social implications of the gospel are clear. However, we will have difficulty implementing them in a society which is blinded by Satanic lies.

It is not that we must refrain from clothing the naked until we have preached to them. Jesus healed and fed and taught all at the same time. Each reinforces the other. But our efforts to alleviate distress will in reality meet with greater success in the degree that society has been delivered from the darkness of the Lie. Social action in itself will never enlighten people. Therefore, the proclamation of the truth must always be our prime focus. We minister aid because we cannot, if we are truly Christian, help doing so. But our goal is to introduce Jesus, the Truth, and he needs to be introduced clearly.

Now whereas there are many forms of social action for which we will not be persecuted, this is not always true about preaching Jesus. Dragged before the Council after healing a lame beggar and preaching about Jesus in the temple grounds, Peter and John make no apology for their defiance of the law. Before an awesome assembly, including such dignitaries as Annas, Caiaphus and other members of the ruling aristocracy, they are faced with a command to desist from preaching Jesus. They reply, "Judge for yourselves whether it is right in God's sight to obey you rather than God. For we cannot help speaking about what we have seen and heard" (Acts 4:19-20). Having heard of the warnings and threats, the whole church prayed with Peter and John for power to defy the authorities. And God answered them with such an outpouring of his Spirit that the building was shaken (Acts 4:31). Clearly God was behind their defiance.

Here the issue is straightforward. They were fulfilling the Great Commission (Mt 28:17-20). The command of Christ was clear and obviously ran counter to the law. But there is no area in which it is easier to make a mistake than in the matter of civil disobedience. We are citizens as well as Christians, and Christians in the past have too frequently hidden from responsibility by seeing it confined to what went on inside church buildings. We are called on to love our neighbors as ourselves, to clothe the naked, feed the hungry, protect the weak.

But history is replete with examples of tragically mistaken enthusiasms, sometimes often involving force. In retrospect, the issues are easier to understand, but at the time the protagonists are utterly convinced. Is revolution ever right? Latin American Christians have often asked the question. Was Oliver Cromwell's attempt to produce a Christian England justifiable? I do not think so, but some Christians today would answer yes.

Violence never solves problems. Neither does force. It may throw out one form of government and institute another. But the second government will turn out in the long run to be little different from the first. Was there really more freedom under Stalin than there had been under the Czars? Tyranny is still tyranny under whatever banner it flourishes.

The task of proclamation, then, must never be neglected. Untruth still holds the world in darkness. The Beast still rules, so the proclamation of the kingdom and the teaching of disciples must remain our first concern. Anything that threatens that commission threatens the whole reason for our existence. Task forces from among the church's membership may rightly take up other concerns, but these must never supersede the Great Commission in importance.

Second, evils within society can be fought on two levels.

One level is the obvious one. Drug addicts must be delivered from addiction and laws formed to minimize drug traffic. The manifest evil must be faced head on. But behind every evil lies the rule of principalities and powers in heavenly places. The problems will never be solved by civil action and new legislation alone. Spiritual warfare (and how little we know about it) plays a far more important role in overcoming evil than does social action. And where should the church's real expertise lie? Surely in the battle in heavenly places!

But my real aim in this chapter is that we should face in our hearts the issue of persecution by the State. How should Christians react when persecution comes? We have already seen that we must live inoffensively. We must never merit punishment for bad behavior. We have also seen that we must do what we can to avoid persecution. We will have to take some risks of course. But as a basic principle we must assume that a living and active witness is better than a dead one.

Many years ago I visited Eastern Europe. I was moved by the love among the Christians whom I met and whom I was helping with Christian literature. Part of their activity was underground because a number of Christians had been imprisoned for carrying out certain activities (baptism, for example) disapproved of by the government. What moved us most was the courage of some of the older women who would spend their afternoons distributing Christian literature. This was, of course, forbidden. To escape detection they would get on a street car, quickly check the passengers with experienced eyes, distribute literature, give a brief public testimony and alight at the next stop. From time to time one would be caught and sentenced to a period in jail. The fun of the game might appeal to the cops-and-robbers instinct in us, but for these women it was a serious way of life. But they used their wits to escape trouble (as we did ourselves).

Ethical problems raise their heads when the church or some of its activities are driven underground. What ought I to have done when my Christian friends asked me to arrange for them to have more literature printed for them bearing a prerevolutionary date? (I didn't, but I think I might do so now.) How are we to understand Paul's and Peter's admonitions to be obedient to civil authorities (Rom 13:1-7; 1 Pet 2:13-17)?

We must recognize then that there are certain imperatives for Christians which no earthly ruler has the right to interfere with. Blessed are Christians who have the courage to defy authority under such conditions and the wisdom to avoid getting caught.

And if you do get caught? If you are brought to trial? Christians experience a number of reactions when they are apprehended for the sake of Christ. Almost all experience extreme anxiety—even fear. This is normal. Others are overwhelmed with self-doubt and a sense of guilt. Prison officers know how to play on the fears and doubts of Christian prisoners with devilish skill.

Christians find themselves asking: "Did I do right? Was I perhaps being too proud? Is the Lord trying to teach me a lesson? Have I not been irresponsible to my family? What will happen to my wife and children? Will my parents be harassed?" The world looks very different from the inside of a prison.

Yet if ever Christians must be firm in suffering, it is after being captured. Two things we must never cease to do are closely related. First, we must not give way to a sense of false guilt or shame, but must praise and glorify God with our hearts and, when there is a chance, with mouths and lungs. (Paul and Silas unintentionally produced a midnight earthquake when they sang praises in prison.) I trust that most people who read these words will never go to prison. But should you go for Christ's sake, trample false shame and guilt under your feet. Lift your head up high. Smile. Treat your jailers with courtesy. Above all, praise and worship God.

The second thing to do is deliberately to entrust your fate to a faithful Creator (1 Pet 4:19). He opens prison doors and has done so repeatedly in the ancient and modern world alike. At other times he has a purpose in keeping his servants locked up. Paul, who was miraculously delivered from prison in Lystra, seems not to have been released in Rome. Yet, from Rome came several of the Epistles. Additionally, John Bunyan's greatest writing was done in jail. For the Holy Spirit generally sees to it that Christians under these circumstances get special help. More than one prisoner has told me that their time for Christ in jail was the happiest time in their life. Christian martyrs have consistently astonished observers by the reality of their joy.

So if death should await you, have no fear. Entrust your soul to him. You will be uplifted and empowered in a way that will cause people around you to shake their heads in wonder.

Questions for Individuals and Groups

1. In what ways have you seen the Holy Spirit at work?
2. When have you seen Christians suffer because of their own errors, rather than for Christ?
3. What examples of Christians being persecuted by governments for their faith do you know of (at home or overseas)?
4. Have you seen our government becoming more intolerant of Christianity? If so, how (pp. 108-109)?
5. When should Christians obey the State and when should they disobey (pp. 109-111)? Can you give examples of each?
6. How does Satan gain power on earth (p. 111)? How does God overcome Satan (p. 111)?
7. When have you waged war with Satan over sin in your life? How did

you overcome the power of sin?

8. Do you agree or disagree with the author's description of the priority of proclaiming the gospel over social action (pp. 113, 115)? Explain. How do you resolve this tension between the two needs in your life?

9. When would you take part (or have you already taken part) in acts of civil disobedience? When should Christians use force or take part in war? In what other ways can Christians be actively involved in battle (p. 109)?

10. How do you feel when you read about Paul praising God from his prison cell? How does this affect your understanding of praise?

9

The
Pathway
of Faith

What might *happen is often more terrifying to think about* than the reality of what will. Yesterday I walked along a lakeshore talking with a friend. He told me of an appeal for total commitment to Christ he had heard in church the day before. He was a devoted and extremely conscientious Christian. Deeply troubled, he confessed to me, "I can't face what he might ask of me. I know in my head that God loves me, but it's just not real to me. And I'm afraid."

He knew all the traditional answers (for instance, "God is gracious and loving" and "God understands your fears"), but fear and doubt gripped him still. His head was convinced, but his heart was troubled. Worse yet, he blamed himself for being the way he was and felt powerless to change and powerless to be changed by God.

He was more honest than many of us. And more realistic

It is harder to face commitment when we are older, and he was married and had children. But some of us have not faced certain possibilities he faced not because we are older, but because deep in our hearts we have decided not to be committed. Others of us share his fears, for we have nightmares of our own. At any rate I am going to assume that some who read these lines may fear the way of the cross.

Some years ago Lorrie, my wife, and I got scared. God had laid it on my heart to expound Revelation 12:1-12 as often as I could. The passage deals with three critical ways in which the feeblest Christian can overcome Satan, and whenever I explained this, Christians were moved and profoundly helped. I also devoted most of a chapter entitled "His Infernal Majesty" in *The Fight* (published by InterVarsity Press) to this passage. But I soon discovered that in preaching and writing about spiritual battles I had gotten myself and my family into our own spiritual battle.

Every time I preached on the passage something major or minor would happen to my wife or to one of the children, usually in the form of a mishap or an accident. At first I thought it must be a series of coincidences. Later it became clearer to Lorrie and to me that no coincidence was involved. Progressively the incidents became more serious. After praying about the matter, Lorrie and I felt clear about our course of action.

We knew that Satan is the "devouring dragon" and "a roaring lion." But we also knew that the only way to overcome him in that capacity was to "love not our lives even unto death."

We determined, along with our children, that we would not back down. For we also had learned that the lion roars more frequently than he devours. His first aim is to intimidate us. He wants to scare us into backing down, and evidently he wanted to stop me from preaching that particular message.

The attacks continued. Some months later I was to preach in St. Margaret's Church in London, England. The church was crowded with African students and others who were studying medicine in the Soviet Union and in other satellite countries, but who had come to Britain to attend a conference organized by the Christian Medical Fellowship. It was a moving occasion, powerfully used by God.

But the same night that I preached in London, Lorrie in Canada was placed in the intensive care unit of a nearby hospital with a severe coronary attack. Her life was in danger. When later the next morning I received a telephone call from my oldest son, I knew exactly what the score was and did some hard thinking.

In spite of the seriousness of Lorrie's condition, I decided to continue at the conference, and to keep in touch by telephone. I was able to speak to Lorrie herself a day or two later, and we agreed that we would still not back down to pressure whatever happened.

But that was the last time we were troubled. A number of years have passed, and never again has there been an attack following my preaching of Revelation 12. I have expounded the passage again and again. Interestingly, Lorrie was divinely healed of her heart condition four years later.

The lesson has come hard, but I am learning that since it is Satan's prerogative to intimidate, it is mine to walk through doors of fear. And when I do so, it is only to discover that in most cases there has been nothing to fear. True, I fight in a real war, and there will be real casualties. But most of our fears will prove unfounded if, sure of our calling, we walk through doors of fear. Let those who fear commitment, then, face the door they must walk through, and take their courage in both hands.

Walking by Faith

Fear and doubt go together. We fear because we are unable to trust. Intellectually we know all the biblical answers. We could counsel someone else with the same fears. But because of our unbelief, our doubts remain. Doubts are—if I may use a golfing cliché—par for the course. It is normal to experience doubt and fear as I face commitment to Christ. Even though I may be experienced in spiritual matters, I may still be assailed by doubt.

Life itself is a gamble. Every decision in life faces us with some degree of risk, and therefore of fear. How can I know anything except by faith? How can I be sure beforehand that I chose the right courses to study? Applied for the right job? How can I be sure that I am about to marry the "right" person—except by faith? And I'm not talking necessarily about faith in God. In life everything I do involves trust in something, even if it is the vague hope/trust that things will work out and be OK.

Business entrepreneurs gamble. Never knowing all the facts, even though they research what they are doing as well as they can, they run risks. In this life we are never in command of all the facts. Risk is involved in all that we do.

Of course some people do not allow themselves to fear, yet their attitude is hardly one of trust—unless it is trust in their own ability. They simply do not let certain possibilities enter their mind. And that is one way to handle the matter.

Last night I saw the leader of the Canadian Snowbirds interviewed on television. He captains a group of jet pilots who give stunning displays of spectacular formation flying. Though the safety record of similar groups is high, accidents are appalling when they do happen.

The captain of the Snowbirds was a squat fire hydrant of a man with twinkling eyes and a relaxed manner. The interviewer asked him about his responsibilities as leader of the group, and he outlined the horrible consequences to the rest of the planes if he made an error in judgment as he led the formation.

"What if you made a mistake?" the interviewer asked

"We don't make mistakes. We can't afford to."

"But if you did?"

"That's something I never allow to enter my mind. I couldn't fly if I did."

Some Christians operate like that. But faith is not the same as "never allowing" something to enter your mind. Faith is not knowing the possibilities, according to human reckoning, but knowing the Person one can trust enough to have confidence in him. That's how other Snowbird pilots related to their captain, whose confidence was in his own skills, concentration and judgment.

For example, many churches and Christian organizations profess to be relying on God for their finances. But in fact they are more commonly trusting in their skills in fund-raising. People like yourself who are facing commitment, either for the first time, or as a matter of re-commitment, are brought face to face with the fact that commitment to Christ means launching at times into open seas where faith really matters. Storms may lie ahead, and your boat is small.

How do we get faith? How much faith is needed?

Very little faith is needed in a life of commitment. All the faith we need is faith enough to obey. I have the impression that Martha, the sister of Mary, had very little faith that Lazarus would rise from the dead. We can't be sure, but the story seems to suggest it. Obviously, she had some faith, though. " 'Lord,' she said to Jesus, 'if you had been here, my brother would not have died. But I know that even now God will give you whatever you ask' " (Jn 11:21-22).

Jesus told her that Lazarus was going to rise again, and her faith seemed promptly to slip. "I know he will rise again in the resurrection at the last day" (Jn 11:24).

At the tombside the test became more severe. "Take away the stone," Jesus commanded, and at once Martha's fears surfaced. "But Lord, . . . by this time there is a bad odor, for he has been there four days" (Jn 11:39).

How much faith did Martha have? Perfect faith? I doubt it. *But she had enough faith to order the stone to be moved.* And that is what matters. Your faith may be small, but it is not too small for you to take a step. And that step is all God expects.

Faith is not like elastic that can be stretched to any limit, but like a muscle that grows with exercise. A walk of faith is a walk in which God exercises that muscle, giving it at each stage a task that seems just a shade too much.

Or, to change the simile, learning faith is like learning to surf. As I mentioned previously, you probably have enough faith to rent a small surfboard and try to body surf nearer the shore. That is all God requires at first. And when he takes you where the big waves are, you will find him riding the bigger waves with you.

Intimacy

Pilots on the Snowbird team know their captain intimately. They have been briefed and debriefed by him many times. They have flown with him for countless hours, have seen and admired his incredible skill as a flier. They have never known him to make a mistake, have sensed his confidence, his relaxed unflappability and have marvelled at the exactness of his judgment.

They have known him off-duty as well as on, observing his character and his open warmth. Their respect for him and their confidence in him have grown with increased closeness.

The more intimate they have become, the more confidently they fly. And this is crucial to their formation flying. For every complex and dangerous maneuver, their eyes must not be on their instruments or on the horizon, but on the leader, on *him*. They must at that point think only on the precise relationship of their aircraft to his. He maneuvers the whole squadron. They must not waste time calculating for themselves what he already has assessed; they simply arrange their position in relation to his.

They trust him with their lives. And they can do so because they know him so well. If you or I were pilots on his team, we might find it easier to trust him—a fallible human being— than to trust Christ. Why? Simply because he's *there*—alive, close and knowable, whereas Christ is someone we have never seen, however much we may have read or heard about him.

I have put it quite bluntly, yet that is the way it often is. We deceive ourselves. We glibly quote Scripture and boast about our confidence in Christ—until he leads us into a dangerous maneuver we have never encountered before, and then we panic. The fact is that it's easier to trust what we can see than what we cannot.

Yet intimacy with Christ is possible, and trust arises out of intimacy. We can know Christ more intimately than the team members know the captain of the Snowbirds. The Holy Spirit was given to us that we might know Christ, and the Father through him, with the greatest degree of intimacy known to humanity. We were made for that purpose.

We were born with a longing for intimacy of a kind no human relationship will satisfy. The longing is buried deep in every human heart, sometimes overlaid by the fears and traumas that life has taught us. But it burns deep within us still.

One way in which that intimacy is developed is in prayerful

waiting on God, and in prayerful meditation in the Scriptures. There are many books which will facilitate your learning, and if you know of none to start with, let me recommend *The Joy of Listening to God* by Joyce Huggett and *Too Busy Not to Pray* by Bill Hybels, both published by InterVarsity Press. And the other way you already know about—learning to trust in the small waves first. It is in *that* way he always leads.

But the first step may be the most intimidating, the step of commitment, of taking up the cross. Let me say at once that if you call on his name he will take you seriously. He offers you his covenant, and if by faith you receive it, the thing is done. Now, change the image from that of a cross to that of a yoke.

Jesus says, "Come to me, all you who are weary and burdened, and I will give you rest. Take my yoke upon you and learn from me, for I am gentle and humble in heart, and you will find rest for your souls. For my yoke is easy and my burden is light" (Mt 11:28-30).

To whom does he call? To the weary and burdened.

What does he offer? A yoke—a light yoke that is easy to carry and links us to him.

What is its purpose? Its purpose is that we learn. Learn to walk with him. Learn, if you like, to surf with him. Or to fly with him. And remember, learning is a process. It may go on for some time after it has begun.

And his invitation—can it be trusted? He responds, "Heaven and earth will pass away, but my words will never pass away" (Mt 24:35).

Questions for Individuals and Groups

1. Have you ever feared that God would call you to a task that is difficult for you to face? Did God ever actually call you to that task? What happened?

2. What do you think is the root of our doubts (pp. 124-125)?

3. Do you agree with the author's statement, "Risk is involved in all that we do" (p. 124)? Why or why not?

4. How do you define faith? How much faith does commitment require (pp. 125-127)?

5. Is there anyone you know whom you trust like the Snowbird pilots trust their captain? Is it easier to trust that person than to trust Christ? Explain.

6. How could you increase your trust in Christ (p. 127-128)?

7. What changes would increased commitment to Christ bring to your life?

10

The First Step
and the
Last

We have discussed many things together. *Some of you who read* may have been experiencing a degree of reorientation in your thinking. I hope this is so. You may have re-evaluated an aspect of your life and your understanding. I have tried to make it plain that the way of the cross, the way of commitment, is a way into freedom. It is a way that majors in joy, even though it involves suffering—in peace, even though it involves conflict—in a growing trust, even though you may struggle with doubt. Above all, it is a journey into intimacy.

Re-evaluation, reorientation and freedom: I have also made it plain that they will begin to take effect in your life when you take a step. For commitment is a journey. The late Chairman Mao has said that a journey of a thousand miles begins with the first step. At this moment there may well be a specific decision you can make which will constitute that first step. God knows what that step is, and he wants to show it to you. If you have not already committed your life to Christ, your first step will be to kneel down and do so.

In Abram's case, the first step was to leave the tiny Chaldean settlement of Haran. Terah, his father, had settled there years before on a pilgrimage that was never completed. The whole family had started out for Canaan. "Terah took his son Abram, his grandson Lot . . . and together they set out from Ur of the Chaldeans to go to Canaan. But when they came to Haran, they settled there" (Gen 11:31-32). They were still there when Terah, Abram's father, eventually died.

Abram had all the feelings you have. He would have wept over his father's corpse. He would have been humiliated over his inability to impregnate Sarai. He would be concerned about his responsibility to his nephew Lot. It was in the middle of sorrow, frustration and responsibility that God's call came, commanding Abram to set out again to a country that he would show him (Gen 12:1).

Sorrow and frustration notwithstanding, there was comfort in Haran. Not only had the family made friends, but extended family connections held them in a comforting network. They would be familiar with the country, with the way of life, and would have a recognized place in the local society. Sacrifice would be involved if Abram were to follow God's word. He would leave his father's remains behind him. His responsibility for Lot's well-being would increase. He would need to find new pastures for his animals and perhaps to relearn the ways and customs of nomadic tribesmen.

God's call to Abram can therefore be seen as a call to make a radical step of commitment. And since the step involved a great cost, it would be a sacrificial commitment.

Yet are we to view the move as an example of sacrificial obedience or as a gamble of faith? For the word that came to him was, "I will make you into a great nation and I will bless you; I will make your name great, and you will be a blessing. . . . all peoples on earth will be blessed through you" (Gen 12:2-3).

Look at it another way. In Haran lay obscurity and eventual oblivion. In the call of God lay an immortal destiny. In packing up his belongings and moving his family across the desert, Abram was taking the first step in what was to become the all-time classic life of faith. He was, in addition, to set in motion a stream of history which would change the Western world for three millennia, allowing Abram to contribute through his descendants more to modern music, drama, science and banking than any other person. These same descendants would remain at the center stage of world history at the end of time. From his loins would spring not only kings and prophets but the redeemer of the world. It is impossible to estimate the effects on human history of Abram's decision to leave Haran.

But Abram had no means of foreseeing, let alone understanding, Einsteinian physics, Rothschild banking or two thousand years of church history. He had but the word of God and the promise of a destiny. His decision to move out, sacrifice or no sacrifice, was essentially a gamble of faith. He trusted God that there were better things for him than lay in Haran.

I do not know what your Haran is. To leave it may be a less traumatic decision than Abram's. But in its way it will be just as momentous. It will be a step into freedom.

In the Caribbean I once watched people catching monkeys by leaving peanuts inside a coconut shell tied to a tree. There was a hole in the coconut shell big enough for the monkey to insert its fingers and grab the nuts, but not big enough for it to withdraw a fist filled with them. Your first step into freedom may involve dropping a few peanuts. Which is it to be—peanuts or a destiny?

For Abram there were many more steps along the journey of faith and commitment. His faith, like our own, tended to be sporadic. His confidence in God's promise seemed to wax and wane, failing altogether in crises of humiliation and shame.

If Abram had anticipated a life of superficial excitement, or even of instant prosperity, he would have been disappointed. Soon after leaving Haran, the famine descended around him, famine so severe that he felt forced to move to Egypt. To go back to Haran was unthinkable, yet the choice to go south was a reluctant one.

Egypt spelled elegance, power and sophistication to Abram, all of which he found menacing. His fears coalesced into an obsession about Sarai, whose beauty had attracted comment wherever they had been. Egyptian rulers could appreciate a woman's beauty. Would they perhaps seize her? Would his life be in danger because of her? Machismo seems to have played no part in his makeup. He may have felt little shame as he instructed Sarai, "Tell them you are my sister. That way both of us will survive" (Gen 12:13 NEB).

His fears proved realistic. Pharaoh's courtiers, anxious to advance in their master's eyes, were quick to see an opportunity of pandering to his well-developed sense of possession and his sensuality. Like the precocious little boys who tempt sailors in foreign ports with stories of their "beautiful girl" contacts, the courtiers hastened to pour exciting descriptions of Sarai's attributes into the ears of Pharaoh. Abram's sister was soon added to the royal collection. Everyone would be delighted—everyone, that is, except Abram and Sarai. And God.

For God had a large stake in the life of a man who would

leave home and kindred on the basis of his promise. Abram's behavior may have been inadequate. From the twentieth century we cannot judge. Certainly, the unheroic figure which he cuts contrasts strangely with the giant-of-the-faith portrait that is commonly painted of him.

But God moved in to rescue him. The plague that afflicted Pharaoh's household, the vision of God that awoke terror in Pharaoh's heart and the restoration of Sarai, are now part of history. In spite of his misdeeds, Abram received vast increases in his herds and was sent on his way ignominiously.

A Mingling of Mud and Marble

We can take heart from the incident. In discovering Abram's weaknesses we discover that we are in the same league with him. Greek heroes and Bible heroes are qualitatively different. We can only identify with Odysseus by fantasizing. But with Abram we can identify realistically. Abram, you see, was a little man who learned to make great decisions so that he eventually enacted a saga of faith/commitment. The fact that he also made a few despicable decisions en route merely shows us that he was not Homeric. He was human.

And how human! Patriarchal pitfalls are glossed over in sermons and books. We seem to have a need to see a Homeric rather than a godly Abram. We busily window-dress his story and make of it a sales display. We not only window-dress; we window-shop. We can admire, without having to buy what we see. Having window-dressed, we can indeed no longer afford to buy. The price is too high. I want, in contrast, to sell you the human Abram, the Abram of the Egyptian affair and of the Hagar/Ishmael debacle. The Egyptian affair, as we have seen, shows his susceptibility to fear. The Hagar incident shows his unbelief and his weakness in giving way too easily to Sarai.

Sarai was deeply disheartened that she could not become pregnant. All God's promises would be meaningless, of course, if Sarai didn't produce. You can't become the father of nations if you don't begin by being the father of one child. Sarai would see herself as a failure and a hindrance not only as a wife but also to the fulfillment of God's promise. In desperation she worked out a compromise and, according to local custom, offered her maid to Abram to sleep with. Any child born to Hagar would be counted as Sarai's (Gen 16:1-3).

It was the kind of compromise we make ourselves. It is so easy to figure out practical ways by which we can make God's promises come true. The end and the means loom larger in our thinking than God does. Faith in God shrivels before uneasy rationalizations which, when put into practice, leave everyone concerned unhappier than they were before and, more important, alienated from God.

What made Abram go to bed with Hagar? Lechery may have made the decision easier but may equally well have played no part. A desire to placate Sarai was probably more important. We are told nothing of his feelings, but the easy way in which he went along with her later plan to be rid of Hagar is shocking. The whole story of the expulsion of mother and son (Abram's own son) into the inhospitable desert is a clear revelation of Abram's weakness (Gen 16:4-6). Nor can there be much question that a disappointing sense of remoteness and unreality of God's promise took away the last resistance to his unhappy courses of action. He was called to walk in steps of faith, but the echo of the call seemed so elusive and distant that his steps faltered.

You are made, Abram, of the same shameful stuff we are made of ourselves. We are glad that the shabby details of your actions have been laid on the line. There was no other way we could know you share with us the mingling of mud and marble that make up a human.

And marble there was as well. The noble decision at Haran to gamble on the promises of an invisible God was a decision Abram made many times over. Though the call could wax faint, it would break into his consciousness repeatedly and with renewed force and clarity. Caught up by the impelling word of God, he would re-enact his Haran decision. Sometimes the word came after he had, in the absence of any strong assurance, acted as he knew he should. Then in the aftermath of the decision, as he stood and trembled at his own temerity, the comfort of reassurance would come.

Such was the case when he gave Lot the first choice of grazing land. The herders of the two men had been at odds over grazing and water. Tensions were growing. As the senior family member as well as the more powerful of the two, Abram could easily have insisted upon some arrangement more advantageous to himself. Instead he told Lot to take his pick of available land. He himself would move family and flocks to whatever area Lot rejected (Gen 12:5-11).

Lot chose the best land. If someone offers you a plum, why not take it? And Abram held firmly to his agreement. On the surface it was nothing more than a generous manner of working out a family problem.

But it was more. God had promised the land to Abram. In offering grazing areas to Lot, Abram was opening the way for Lot to stake claims in the very area he himself hoped one day to possess. Was he weak and confused, or was he demonstrating extraordinary faith in the promise? It seems to me that where family duty (remember, Abram had a responsibility toward Lot) and his own ambitions for the future came into conflict, he chose loyalty and trusted God to look after the consequences.

My intuition is borne out by the fact that twice in the years that followed, Abram went out on a limb to save Lot. One occasion involved a hazardous rescue attempt (Gen 14:12-16), while another involved, as Abram saw it, jeopardizing his own relationship with God (Gen 18:20—19:29). Yet Abram risked his life, his future and even God's favor to intervene on Lot's behalf. Abram might make mistakes. He might be too eager to please Sarai. Yet his attitude toward Lot revealed his deep faith in God's promise.

The Last Step on the Way of the Cross

So far in this chapter I have tried to make a number of things clear. First, I have been careful to point out that Abram's sacrificial commitment to God is best seen not as sacrifice but first as a step, then as a journey, of faith. Second, I have tried to show that there was nothing extraordinary about the man himself. He had serious flaws. Third and most important, Abram's journey of faith can only be understood if we see it as a response to the reiterated call and repeated promises of God.

And something more. Remember our discussion of intimacy in the last chapter? Faith grows with intimacy, and God was offering Abram friendship.

How that call and those promises came to him is immaterial. Whether they came in the form of auditory voices or an inner conviction is actually beside the point. If God exists and if God wants to communicate with a person, he may choose any vehicle through which to communicate. Of one thing we may be sure. If God wants to get something across, he will. And the glory of the God of the Scriptures is that he longs to communicate—not only to an Abram but to all his servants. The story of Abram is recorded because it can be your story. For God sees you as his servant and as his child.

Two incidents stand out that reinforce the strange inter-
action between God's word and the faith of Abram (or Abraham, as he was later named). The more disturbing of the two,
and certainly the climax and the greatest turning point of his
life, was the sacrifice of his promised son, Isaac (Gen 22:1-18).
Nowhere else in the Bible does God command human sacrifice. Indeed the sacrifice by parents of their offspring is
singled out as being abhorrent to God. Why did God command Abraham to do something he hated?

We must be clear on two points. Abraham would not share
our modern feelings about human sacrifice. That is to say, it
would present him with no moral problem. Whatever feelings
of dread and sorrow he might struggle against, there would
never occur to him the idea that human sacrifice was in itself
evil. It was the accepted practice of his day. If it meant anything to him, it would signify a proof of devotion to his God.

The second point arises from this fact. Knowing how Abraham would view the command (that is, as an act of devotion),
God, we read, tested Abraham. Would Abraham (not a twen-
tieth-century person, but a child of a dark age where the
offering of one's children to God in sacrifice was the ultimate
proof of love and trust) trust God enough to obey the command? Having waited years for the impossible—a child from
his own and Sarah's bodies—could he trust God to keep the
promise made at Haran, a promise repeated many times
since?

Abraham's decision to sacrifice Isaac represents the last
step of his journey. If we view it as a commitment, his commitment is now complete. If we view it as faith (where the
true heart of the matter lies), his trust in God is great enough
now to fly in the face of instinct and common sense. So much
is he prepared to gamble on the word of God that he gets
ready to plunge a knife into the body of his own boy, because

he "reasoned that God could raise the dead" (Heb 11:19).

The knife was raised but God intervened. Abraham's bewildered eyes saw a living ram caught in a thicket beside him. His ears heard the now-familiar voice telling him to release the ropes that bound his son to the altar. God's purpose was accomplished. He had taught a human to trust him.

And this is all he wants to teach you. Whether you hear him or not he is calling you. Tune out other clamoring sounds. In the depths of your spirit he waits to meet you. Let there be no doubt in your mind, he is going to extraordinary lengths to communicate with you.

Years before the climactic scene by the altar, God had spoken to Abraham in terms that Abraham could not possibly have mistaken. The local custom in making a contract called for an unusual ceremony. An animal would be divided in half and the two halves laid a few feet apart. Parties to the contract would walk between the divided remains of the animal. In doing so they were saying by the symbol, "May my body be cut in half, in the way this animal's body is, if I should betray my word and break my covenant." Such a contract was exceedingly solemn and binding.

Even before Abram's name was changed to Abraham, God made exactly this sort of covenant with him. Abram was instructed to take five living creatures (signifying the extreme solemnity of the occasion)—a heifer, a female goat, a ram, a dove and a pigeon, and to divide the animals (the heifer, the goat and the ram) in half, laying them out according to the prescribed covenant ritual (Gen 15:1-10).

At the time Abram had grave doubts about God's promise to him. His faith was low. Nevertheless, he laid out the animals in the accepted manner and waited. Hours passed. Vultures descended from time to time to seize the dead flesh, and Abram was obliged constantly to drive them away. Slowly the sun went down, and as it did so a nightmare-like trance passed over Abram. Further revelations of God's will were made to him. Then, in the darkness a glowing brazier and a flaming torch appeared, symbolizing the presence of God. Both the brazier and the torch passed between the divided halves of the dead animals. "To your descendants," the voice came, "I give this land" (Gen 15:11-21). The whole incident constituted a seal that any nomad of that age would understand.

You say you wish God would go to such pains to speak to you? Stand at Golgotha as the horror of darkness falls. Look at the God-man who hangs in extremity from a gallows. Dare you demand further evidence of God's good will in his negotiations with you? The brazier and the torch have passed between the animals. God has committed himself. He has spoken the irrevocable word for your comfort and your assurance.

Perhaps you are waiting as the sun goes down. Perhaps vultures would snatch away the evidence that any contract exists between you and God. Go to the Scriptures. Read in the Gospels all that took place. Spend time meditating, letting the Holy Spirit speak to you from the passages. Christ's body was of human flesh and it was lifted up on a cross. The darkness actually descended. The veil in the temple was torn in two. These things happened and were recorded that you might know God has committed himself to anyone who trusts him. He has gone to great pains to assure you that the gamble of faith is no gamble; that your commitment, your sacrifice, your step of faith will represent an entry into a deeper relationship with himself. The cost to you is trivial. What he offers is of far greater value. But you must believe— enough to take some specific step.

If you are uncertain, be in no hurry to decide what that step is. Do not move from Haran in fevered panic. Wait before God in silence. Are there pressures and frustrations? Go to the tabernacle within yourself where God abides in stillness. Tell him you worship him. He will speak since he is more anxious to reach you than you are to be reached.

He is in fact already speaking. It is only necessary that you learn to listen.

Questions for Individuals and Groups

1. The author says that commitment involves "re-evaluation, reorientation and freedom" (p. 131). In your own words, what do each of these mean? What changes does each bring to your life?

2. Have you ever taken a difficult step as Abram did when he went to Haran? What sacrifices were involved in taking it? What blessings?

3. How do you feel when you read the account of Abram and Sarai (pp. 134-136)? When have you seen God's faithfulness in your life in spite of your own faithlessness?

4. Have you ever taken it upon yourself, as Sarai did (p. 136), to make sure that God's promises come true? What happened?

5. What does the story of Abram and Lot (pp. 137-138) tell you about Abram? If we are like Abram, then how does this story make you feel about yourself?

6. How has God worked in your life to teach you to trust him?

7. How has God shown you that he is committed to you?

8. Following in Abram's path, what first step is God asking you to take? If you are unsure, how can you learn to listen to his voice (p. 142)?

Notes

[1]William Shakespeare, *Henry VIII*, IV, iii, 217.
[2]C. S. Lewis, *The Pilgrim's Regress* (Grand Rapids: Eerdmans, 1958), p. 24.
[3]Arthur S. Booth Clibborn, "There Is No Gain."
[4]"And Can It Be," words by Charles Wesley.
[5]Michael Kinsley, "Thatcher for President" in *Time*.
[6]C. S. Lewis, *The Problem of Pain* (New York: Macmillian, 1977), p. 16.
[7]John White, *The Fight* (Downers Grove, Ill.: InterVarsity Press, 1976), p. 115.
[8]Lewis, *The Problem of Pain*, p. 81.
[9]Samuel W. Gandy, "I Hear the Accuser Roar," in *The Believers' Hymn Book* (London: Pickering and Inglis).
[10]Ibid.